# HONEY & VINEGAR
## RECIPE FOR AN OUTLAW
a memoir by Sossity Chiricuzio

Beaten Track
www.beatentrackpublishing.com

Honey & Vinegar: Recipe for an Outlaw

Published 2019 by Beaten Track Publishing
Copyright © 2019 Sossity Chiricuzio

All rights reserved.

No part of this publication may be reproduced, stored in a retrieval system, or transmitted, in any form or by any means, without the prior permission of the publisher, nor be otherwise circulated without the publisher's prior consent in any form of binding or cover other than that in which it is published and without a similar condition including this condition being imposed on the subsequent publisher.

The moral right of the author has been asserted.

Paperback ISBN: 978 1 78645 371 6

eBook ISBN: 978 1 78645 372 3

Beaten Track Publishing,
Burscough, Lancashire.
www.beatentrackpublishing.com

## Art Credits

Cover design by Debbie McGowan. Illustrated by Queeriam, a fellow desert rat poor kid grown into an outlaw artist who was able to capture the spirit of my stories in magical lines of ink and intention. Artist adult photo by J Tyler Huber Photography, because there is no gaze like that of another femme, and child photo by one of the good men I am so grateful to have had in my life, Clyde Brazil.

# Introduction

We are a family of stories, stitched together into a patchwork quilt, made up of yard sale finds and hand-me-downs and free box treasures. This is an accurate indication of our economic reality, but if you think this is about pity, you miss the point entirely. Our family knows how to make magic out of making do. Survival is an art.

# Notice

*Honey & Vinegar* is a work of creative nonfiction about my life, however, names have been omitted or changed to respect privacy and personal wishes. There is never just one truth to a lived experience that is shared, so this is my story, told from my perspective, and not intended to speak for or define the story of anyone else.

# Dedication

This book is dedicated to generation upon generation of peasant women on various continents in my family line, who labored and loved, kept families together and fed, and were known on occasion to apply outlaw solutions to traditional problems. It is dedicated to their descendants, many of whom have turned outlaw solutions into family traditions.

It is dedicated to the family of outlaws I have chosen and been chosen into, keeping one another fed and loved and seen despite every way the traditional world tries to disappear us.

It is dedicated to my outlaw partner, Max, and all the traditions we're building around creating art and growing love in nontraditional ways.

And finally, it is dedicated to the femmes in my life, who have shown me what outlaw can look like and how it can change the world. I have so much love and respect and gratitude for you all.

*"Yes, there are two paths you can go by,
but in the long run,
there's still time to change the road you're on."*

*– Led Zeppelin*

# Contents

1. Web of women ........... 3
2. A certain twinkle ........... 6
3. The world tastes like ........... 10
4. Me vs. the pledge of allegiance ........... 11
5. Building a family ........... 13
6. Samantha has ideas ........... 16
7. Make magic with my crayons ........... 17
8. Sorrowful feel good ........... 21
9. Good guys ........... 22
10. Research ........... 24
11. Nowhere to go that is quiet ........... 25
12. Mama makes adventures / Daddy has magic eyes ........... 30
13. Mermaid practice ........... 32
14. Three in the hand ........... 36
15. Poetry and puberty ........... 37
16. Summertime ........... 40
17. The house that crumbled ........... 41
18. First day ........... 47
19. We need the dream ........... 49
20. Monsoon ........... 52
21. Shoulder to shoulder ........... 53
22. Tired of have not ........... 55
23. My high school sweetheart ........... 57
24. Rite of passage ........... 61

| 25. | If I remembered their names | 64 |
| 26. | Red dust under my feet | 68 |
| 27. | Road trip | 69 |
| 28. | Gateway | 74 |
| 29. | Threshold | 77 |
| 30. | Sanctuary | 81 |
| 31. | Single wide trailer | 85 |
| 32. | Up a tree | 86 |
| 33. | Queer activist training camp | 90 |
| 34. | Where secrets always lodge | 93 |
| 35. | Fault lines | 95 |
| 36. | Brown-eyed girl | 101 |
| 37. | Radical sex | 103 |
| 38. | The high cost of education | 106 |
| 39. | Heartsister | 110 |
| 40. | Gentlebutch | 111 |
| 41. | Meeting at the crossroads | 113 |
| 42. | Last night in town | 114 |
| 43. | Stars and steam | 116 |
| 44. | Thunderstorm | 117 |
| 45. | Meditation in motion | 121 |
| 46. | A twisting path | 122 |

# HONEY & VINEGAR

# Web of women

As a teenager in the 1940s, my grannie Iris is, more than once, caught sneaking into the house in the wee hours. She goes to the jazz clubs – specifically forbidden and absolutely compelling. Her mother is worried about smoking, about men, about improper behavior and the so-frequent consequences. What Iris wants, though, is the music. She lives in music, records and radio and foot-tapping on the sidewalk. I don't know what danger she might have found in the jazz clubs, but I doubt it would've narrowed her life any more than marrying that Italian boy did. True to form, he is charming and generous and hard-handed and quick to judge. He has the best of intentions and a bad temper. He loves his children and models hating themselves. He is her husband, but not her match. They are stuck in place and grinding each other down.

Four children to raise and a world awakening to options around her, she goes against church and tradition and divorces him. With the usual way of family separations and personal awakenings, there are rough waves. He takes the youngest son with him to California, as the son is developmentally disabled and needs more resources than a single mother will have. The other three siblings are upheaved into sudden freedom and scarcity all at once. Iris is working full time and also having her own sexual revolution, getting attention from the cowboys for her blue, blue eyes and exploring in several directions at once. She works in a doctor's office and sometimes brings home drug samples – nothing intended to get you high, but thanks to the *Physicians' Desk Reference*, my mother

## SOSSITY CHIRICUZIO

Rose and her friends can look up ones with "interesting" side effects to try out, and often do. That's not what gets my mother expelled from high school, though.

Rose is already tagged as a troublemaker: for protesting when they measure the length of her skirt, for protesting the Vietnam War wearing tire sandals and a black armband, for protesting against being silenced as a girl. Smart, chubby, bespectacled, and vocal, she is impossible to ignore or disguise. She is on the school paper, and she and her coeditors work the words "Fuck the Draft" into the big, ornate, sixties-style border. They get away with it too, but where's the fun in that? One of the boys tells a friend, the word gets around, and the next day my mother is sent to the principal's office.

He explains that the two boys were expelled and that she's going to be suspended for two weeks. When she asks why there is a difference in their punishment, he says that he's sure they talked her into it. She calmly explains it was her idea and her artwork. If he is going to suspend her, he has to suspend them, and if he is going to expel them, then he has to expel her as well. He does, and she gets on with the more relevant aspects of life, like art, and activism, and me.

Rose is carrying on a family tradition, if a bit early – our line is a fertile one. A mother at seventeen in 1970, she commences to work on finding herself, finding community, and finding peace with her own mother. She stands stronger for protecting me, for being loved by me. I am being raised by a web of women, all of them fiercely independent, weaving around me with shared joy. My aunt Poppy, a womanchild herself, shares all the attention and anything she ever tries to eat. Perched on her lap like a baby bird, or hand in sticky hand at the ice cream parlor, I know that I'll never go hungry.

Poppy is the youngest, often baffled by the shifting family dynamics and wishing for the comfort of certainty. She finds happiness in dancing, in the feel of the wind through her long, black hair, in changing her name to suit herself. She is generous to the bone, though sometimes left feeling lonesome for all the giving. She gathers children in like flowers and talks to them like people. Our family is all just people together. A matriarchy, perhaps, but not a hierarchy. Respect is earned with respect, not simply living the longest.

These women and so many others show me the beauty and strength in survival. How to make our home into art, and art into a place to live. How to feed everyone, including myself. They fill our houses with plants to remind us to breathe and grow. They know how to find adventure and joy that is free. They teach me how to feed ten people with two potatoes and make it taste good. Make it last a bit longer. They teach me the difference between being self-sufficient and being stubbornly proud, sometimes while learning the lesson themselves. The need to apply magic and elbow grease both. They teach me every day.

# A certain twinkle

My mom is sixteen and looking for work. She stops into the local Der Wienerschnitzel to fill out an application and meets Clay. Blue eyes, shaggy honey-colored hair and this tilted head grin she can't stop trying to invoke, he is charming and funny and invites her to stick around after the shift for a toke. Of course she does, and they have so much fun that he invites her back to his place. The next morning they pass the bong while watching a new kids' show, *Sesame Street*, which turns out to be perfect stoned viewing, funny and kind and full of fantastical beings. Since they are teenagers, the show loses their interest before it is over, and they fall back into each other. The spark of life that becomes me tumbles

into being in their young passion on that wool blanket, with a high cloud of smoke and a cast of loving characters modeling good behavior in the background.

I don't know if what they had was love, but I do know that my mom wanted me. Wanted a baby, a family of her own. Not a husband; she wasn't looking for that at all, but now she's seventeen and pregnant, and he's leaving for Basic Training, and he and her mother bring the tough love to bear. Marry him, and she'll have benefits and help with the baby. Knowing she needs help, knowing also that he'll be gone soon and for a long time, ready to stop fighting and focus on growing me, she accedes. Even with help she ends up in the County Hospital when her labor starts, alone and unprepared in a cubicle made of hanging curtains in a long, narrow ward. There's nothing to see but hospital drab all around her and a handmade sign someone taped to the ceiling that says "Just keep breathing."

Despite all this, she's excited, feeling good in her body and ready for this experience. A doctor comes through and brusquely checks her dilation. She feels like it will be soon and tells him so. He cuts her off and says she's not ready, it'll be a few hours yet, and leaves her alone again. He's wrong. Her water breaks, she dilates fast, and she ends up giving birth with the help of the ward nurse. It's painful and stressful, but she's strong and determined and so ready to hold me. I finally slip out, and the nurse cleans us both up, but as Rose reaches out for me, the nurse snaps, "You're not sterile!" and bustles me away. Vulnerable, heartbroken, my mom doesn't see me for six hours. Despite it all, we bond immediately, the most familiar heartbeats in the whole world.

There's only one photo of him and me. His clean-shaven, high-boned cheeks and square shoulders, all bent toward me, tiny and bundled and eyes half closed. The walls behind us are empty and beige, and a woman's hands are visible to the left, having just let me go, or waiting to take me back. His face is in profile, and I've never quite been able to read his expression. Is he excited? Terrified? He's just nineteen, headed for a war in Vietnam he knows almost nothing about, married and a father against all his own plans. Is he grieving? Relieved to be going away? Lost in wonder? We've never discussed it, not that we've had much time.

They divorce while he is still overseas. When he comes home, he brings a new wife and son with him. They live in Arizona, near his parents, and I visit once when I'm seven. Once, when I'm eleven, in the summer, I visit all the far-flung family. I stay with his parents, this third set of grandparents that most kids don't have. They are kind strangers with a quiet house. I read books and wait for something to click – with them, with him. There's no sudden rush of emotion, no dramatic connection. He is the man who helped my mom make me, and they made him. They hug me, but he doesn't.

Or if he does, I don't remember. He takes me to work with him, and I feel the awkward go solid. These people don't know who I am or just learned recently. One of them gives me a pen set, or maybe he does. It's a blur of strangeness and feeling like all the strange is me.

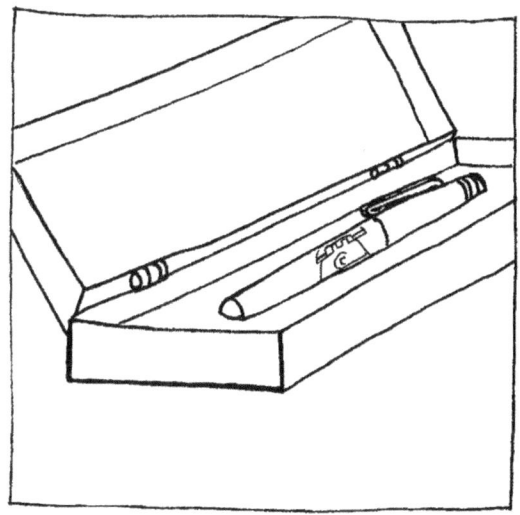

He's a good man, I can tell, doing good work in the world with the telephone union. He's nice to me, but there has been too much time, too much distance, not enough knowing. I don't need another dad; he doesn't need a daughter. Our lives are separate and full. This is no fairy tale of running across the meadow and weeping in his arms; the blood is not a magnet. I know I remind my mother of him, more than just the coloring and stature, more than genetics can explain. A certain spike to my humor, the ability to get right in under someone's nerve. The ability to defuse the chaos that can follow. A generosity. A tendency to procrastinate. A certain twinkle.

# The world tastes like

The sun-warmed leather of my mother's purse strap, fragrant and comforting between my teeth. Kefir, strawberry or peach, at the end of the co-op shift. Sipped for blocks, each mouthful thick with joy. Like steak, that first bite, raw and rich and placed on my tongue by the down-reaching arms of my mother, face high above me alight with the taste of it. Peanut butter, coconut, and carob frozen into dessert, or something close to it. Shrimps curled into pink succulence, brown rice, root beer float.

Smell of rattlesnake hide, curing in the backyard, salvaged from the highway. Creosote and rain on the dust. Incense and butter candles, cinnamon toasting on oats, basil and thyme simmering tomatoes into love. My mother's hair across my face while she rocks me, her skin after work, after sleep, salt on honey. Late-night smoke curls past my window, woody and soft. Wildflowers, rose hips, sandalwood, patchouli, gardenia, wet rocks on the sill.

Sun-dried apples. Easter Peeps left to harden. Sausage links. Tofu baked brown and crisp. Popcorn, but only with nutritional yeast. Mushrooms but not olives. Never broccoli, never liver, always chicken, always potatoes. Fresh green heaps of spinach cooked down to richness. Corn cobs buttered hot, home-baked bread, chips, no dip. Ketchup spun into the carpet but not on my fries. Piles of rejected vegetables, butter and sugar sandwiches, government cheese. Red snapper fins, fried crisp. Tuna noodle casserole. Savory grits, belly full.

# Me vs. the pledge of allegiance

I am excited to go to kindergarten, even though I'm not sure about the whole stay-dressed-all-day thing. All day. And in the same clothes! My mom let me pick my own outfit, so I have on my favorite fancy dress that I got brand-new. It is long and white with pleats and blue roses and tiny buttons and a tie at the waist. I wear it with my brown hiking boots with the red laces that are just like Grannie's. When I go visit her this summer, we're going to climb in the mountains, so I need to break them in. Besides, they feel really strong, and school is new and a tiny bit scary. Except they have their own special library with hundreds of books. I love books.

It turns out that school is kind of like shared childcare, only with fewer adults and more kids. Kids my own age. I should be excited about this, but I'm used to hanging out with adults. I'm not sure what to talk to other kids about. My mom says almost everyone feels shy sometimes, so it's good to say hi first if you feel like you can, and I decide to try at recess. After the teacher gets everyone settled and shows us where things are, she calls out all our names from a list, to make sure we're all here. She says this is roll call and that she'll do it every morning. After roll call, we'll do the Pledge of Allegiance. I can hear the capitals in the words, and I wonder what it is. I know a pledge is a promise, but what are we promising?

She recites the pledge for us and gives us a copy so we can take it home to practice with our parents. I read well for my age, books have always been my comfort zone, and I'm puzzling over the bigger words. I ask my mom about it later, and we talk about promises and government and religion, and I ask why we would be promising to god at school. Isn't that what people do at church? She agrees and says lots of people argue about whether religion belongs in schools. We talk about different kinds of religions and different kinds of promises and agree that I should sleep on it and decide in the morning. She's raised me with spirituality but not religion, though I am encouraged to explore anything that draws me. What I know of church makes me uncomfortable, and I don't want to promise anything I don't believe in, so in the morning I tell her I don't want to say the pledge.

We talk about how to be respectful and how I should talk to my teacher and that she should call my mom if she has any questions. My mother has raised me to negotiate for myself, but it has to make sense. No throwing a tantrum and calling it a discussion. At school, after roll call, we all stand up to do the pledge. I don't put my hand on my heart, because that feels like a promise too, but I do like we discussed and then sit down with everyone else. When it is time for recess, my teacher calls me over to her desk. She asks if I had trouble with the words and I shake my head no. She asks if I'm feeling shy, and I shake my head again. I try to explain that I'm still not sure about god and that I don't feel comfortable promising what the pledge seems to say, that I talked to my mom about it and we agreed I need to be quiet and respectful, but I don't have to say it. My teacher sits there looking at me for a while with her forehead all wrinkled up, then just sends me out to play with the other children, though I think maybe she doesn't really want me to.

# Building a family

There's hardly a photo of me under the age of six with clothes on. Accessories, yes. Shoes, yes. Hats, gloves, purses, glasses, jewelry, even ponchos, but not clothes. Some part of this is being raised by flower children in the 1970s, and some part of it is that the women in my family recognize that we are mammals, that the feel of the sun and grass and wind on our skin is joyful and a treasure.

Comfort in yourself, group discussions, and meditation are the examples that are set. We live in co-housing, multiplexes, row apartments, group houses, communes, ashrams, and once, briefly, a school bus. Sometimes with family, always community,

and eventually with a father. Rose meets and marries the only man I ever called Daddy, surprising them both on their third date. Turned out I was right. Jasper is from Florida, and his long hair comes close to getting him disowned on more than one drunken occasion. Italian earth mama and southern gentleman – it is a strange mix, but it works.

His family welcomes us in, though they find me precocious and my mother unsettling. On our first visit, my new grandmother Ruby runs out to scold us about the Spanish moss we have draped over our heads like a veil while dancing around in the huge beautiful trees on their property. I can tell she is genuinely worried about the burrowing bugs that live in the moss but also that she really wants us to stop doing it where people can see us. Ruby wins me over with chicken and dumplings and sweetness and intricate bits of peacock decor, though her husband Flint first baffles and then scares me.

His end-of-day drunk sometimes gets sloppy, and shame is his ace card. He eventually kicks me off his lap for good when puberty hits at nine, one more man in the world who sees my body more clearly than my childhood, and our tenuous connection is stretched even thinner. Flint isn't dangerous in the way those other men are, but like them, he makes me feel like I'm not actually in the room. He's background noise to the visits anyhow. He really would rather be fishing.

I am five when my sister is born, then a brother when I'm eight and another when I'm ten. They are my siblings and also my pack of kids. Not only because my folks often work swing shifts and then it is just us after school but because I had such a head start. I think of myself as more of a small adult, and mostly so do they. We have a routine, and we get it all done, but we have fun too,

playing with Legos and Matchbox cars and Barbies and blocks and Little People for hours.

I build waist-high forts out of sheets that span the entire front of the house, and for once, everyone has their own room. I build shelves and walls out of stools and game boards, and we drag all our favorite toys and pillows and blankets and stuffed animals and snacks inside and try not to bump the clothespins and thumbtacks that hold it all together. I put a fan in the entrance, and the sheets billow up into gentle waves above us. Strawberry Shortcake and He-Man and flowers and clouds and Tonka trucks and bubbles and stripes, faded and familiar, like a sky of dreams.

# Samantha has ideas

Red hair rumpled, eyes alight with mischief, she is sunlight in the afternoons and a warm hand curled around mine. The discovery of pleasure, exploring and safe and threaded through with laughter. Full of ideas and adventure.

The sweet crunch of cashews and carrots in sandwich bags, sticky in the summer heat. She is a cartoon brightness and the shivery feelings of the lady singing on the Pink Floyd album. Strong like the boys but picks me anyhow.

A few short months of feeling just right, of feeling love that is different than family, that is just for me. She is here, and then she is gone. Glowing like a star behind my closed eyelids, impossible to see in the light of the new day.

# Make magic with my crayons

I'm sitting on the floor at my grandmother's house, picking out colors to use for the first picture in my new fairy coloring book. "All You Need is Love" is playing, and in my head I can picture the green apple going around and around. I watch it sometimes, finding it soothing like the breathing practices I learned when we were staying in that ashram earlier this year. It's something the adults do for meditation, but I like to do it during my everyday stuff. It feels good. I picture my breath coming into my lungs and back out again like a spiral, slow and steady. Green in, blue out. I think about the spirals and start drawing them on the hem of the fairy's skirt. I'm here to visit for a whole month, all by myself, and her house feels really different. Quiet.

## SOSSITY CHIRICUZIO

Our house always has at least the four of us but usually more. Me, my mom, my new dad, and my baby sister. Most of the time, there's also an aunt or uncle or a friend or three. There's lots of shared childcare, so there are usually at least a few little kids around. I'm the oldest, always. There weren't any kids in our group until I was about five, but I'm seven now, and lots of things are different. Grannie's VW Beetle isn't different, though. It still looks like that highest part of the sky on a summer day when the clouds are too tired to float and the blue is all stretched out. It rumbles like a bumblebee, especially on the highway up the mountain to where she lives now.

She tells me stories while she drives, about the fairies that live in the flowers and help the bees. She says there is a fairy in every flower, and I try to imagine that many fairies, but I can't. I'm looking at fields of wildflowers, so many I can't even tell where the edges are. I get really quiet, and Grannie understands. It's like a metaphor, she says. Fairies are the spirit of the flowers, of all the good that flowers have inside. They make the flowers more real because then they have a face like ours. She said it's good to learn to see things with different kinds of faces, but we have to start somewhere.

Grannie has a husky voice from smoking. I hate the smoking. I wish she wouldn't do it, but Mama says it's her choice. I agree with having choices, but I keep hearing how dangerous it is, how it can make you really sick. I'm reading a Ramona Quimby book, and in the story her dad smokes and she hates it too. She and her sister Beezus take his pack and pull out all the cigarettes and throw them away. They make twenty notes about how they love him and want him to be healthy and put them in the pack where the cigarettes go. He's mad at first but ultimately he listens and promises to try to stop. I think this is a good plan and decide to give it a try.

I prepare carefully, making my notes ahead of time because I want to do it while she naps, and that's only about forty-five minutes. I use my favorite colors and try to use logic too. I carefully slide the cigarettes out but decide not to throw them away. I'm not sure this will work and I know it's wrong to break something that isn't yours, especially if you can't replace it. I roll the notes up tight and push them into place, and then sneak the pack back onto the table on the porch. She always smokes outside, because secondhand smoke is bad. All smoke is bad, I think, but grown-ups are stubborn.

When she wakes up from her nap, I listen for the back door. About five minutes after she goes out, I hear it again, and then she's standing over me. It's all over my face, and she sits down on the couch near me.

"Where are they?"

I stall.

"Did you read the notes?"

She lifts her eyebrow at me. This isn't going like the Ramona book at all, and I start to tear up.

"I just don't want you to get sick!" I'm whining, ruining the calm voice I want to be using, and she sighs.

"I understand, honey, but it's complicated. It's my choice, and you have to respect it. You can't take other people's things, even if you think you're right."

I pull the cigarettes from their hiding place and lay them across her palm. She gives me a hug, and then takes them back out onto the porch with her. She doesn't give back the notes, though.

The record finishes side B and flips over again, and I imagine Lucy in the Sky with Diamonds as a fairy, and she makes all the cigarettes disappear without making anybody sad. I color the fairy in flower shades and try again to make magic with my crayons.

# Sorrowful feel good

Deep vibrations under my feet from the amp, enormous, they stand me upon. Ten years old and in love with the blues. Setting my skin alight with sorrowful feel-good.

Like waves of hope in a sea of tears that I'm not crying. Music too strong, pulling my eyes shut. The better to glory in red and blue light shows inside the lids, fluttering like all of me.

On stage, Bo Diddly. Hands like a thunderstorm, though they were gentle when I shook them backstage. Before I knew he was a magician. Turning a guitar into a sword. A feast. A blessing.

# Good guys

The men I grow up with are so different from the men I encounter out in the world. My uncle Rowan with his long red hair blowing in the wind while he plays guitar at my parents' wedding is an image I can conjure up with ease. Sunlight and acoustic Cream and snap-front shirts and laughter. Wry humor and a masterful eyebrow. He always has time for a question or a hug, even if his pretty girlfriends are waiting. He puts other men at ease, and women too. He drives a classic bug, rides a motorcycle, plays the bass guitar, and prints books. Pretty much the coolest everything. He treats me like I'm precious but not a princess, and I'm not. I'd much rather be a teacher anyway or a jockey or a doctor for wild animals. Whatever it is, he agrees I can do it, and I believe him.

My dad's army buddy Fritz and I understand each other, too. We are both watchers, hanging out at the edges of the circle and seeing all the ways patterns form and shift. We like to figure out how things work, including people. He had been struck by lightning and has no sense of smell or taste left, and his skin is sensitive even to a shower. That wasn't the first time he almost died. He was ill and in bed for many years as a child, and his ribcage is boxy from being compressed while growing. When he first told me that story, I was seven. I thought of him, slowly rotating in his bed over the course of a day, wall, ceiling, wall, and started to cry. He told me he spent the time reading and that he had read more books than anybody he ever knew. Knowing that books are the greatest escape, I was comforted.

He was in the war with my father. They sent messages by Morse code about where the other ships and troops were. They manage to make it sound like an adventure when they talk about it at all, avoiding any discussion of guns or fighting, never speaking ill of the people they had fought. It takes me years of my own exploration and reading to find out just what kind of conditions they were in every day, what they were being asked to do and risk. My gentle father and his gentle friend, soldiers. It makes no sense. My dad will sometimes do our names in Morse code, turning us into a pile of giggles with his dit dot dit dot dot dot dit dot dot dot dot. As I get older, I realize those same letters that make up our names also gave away a position for bombing or pinpointed a spot to avoid. I think about how intensely that training sticks with him, more than a decade later. It is surely not the only lasting effect.

All these men are family to me, are safety, are comfort. They pick me up and carry me around, but only when it's fun or helpful. They give me balls and dolls and cars and tops and crayons and paint and books. They are gentle with me and silly at times, with their long beards and belly laughs. They are sweet to their sweethearts, take turns doing dishes and changing diapers and washing clothes. They make art. They make music. They make the women in my family happy. This is what I know of men, before the one who comes in disguise and steals what I hardly knew was mine. Before public school and television and puberty and the drunk guys at the park on the way home and the flasher outside the mall and so many others make it clear that I live with the good guys and that they are rare.

# Research

I love libraries. Rooms full of books, made just for books, with answers waiting to be found. Stories and legends and science and magic. Love and sorrow and laughter and mystery. Safety. There's no shouting or pushing or competing allowed. No little kids yelling, no grown-ups too busy to talk. Just helpful librarians and other people reading. Just the world I pick. Like a coloring book in my mind, I fill in the details, and the hero can look like me.

The smell of books, the hidden alcoves at the ends of rows, the formed plastic chairs like a cupped hand. My legs going numb from dangling over the hard lip of the seat, my shoulders and head all curved into the world between those covers. Squinting in the light when it flickered, automatically, all attention inward. Almost locked in more than once, so that the librarians learn to check for me in the depths of physical sciences or psychology, all the books nobody tends to read, before leaving.

I read the entire Alice in Wonderland series, not just the first part that they made all soft for Disney; the real story. The conflict and the angst and the tension. The confusion. The real stuff dressed up as fiction. I read every book of mythology and find some hints of comfort in goddesses and amazons and warrior queens. I'm looking for the women who aren't afraid. The girls who are smart. The way out. I travel to Narnia and Pern and Mars and am still disappointed when I get there. It still ends in a kiss I don't want. A man who knows more. A woman who is a support beam. A cook stove. A baby carriage.

A stranger in a strange land. A woman on the edge of time. The last unicorn.

# Nowhere to go that is quiet

We're moving to Florida, where Dad's family lives. Not right where they live by the Pensacola Bay, but more in the middle. A city called Gainesville, where Mom and Dad can both find work and we can swim all year. A city that is seven states away, even if Oklahoma

just kind of sticks out a bit along the way, and then down, toward the ocean. In fact, it's surrounded by ocean on three sides, which is a lot of water, and is also full of rivers and springs and lakes. I wonder if all the houses are really close together, or up on stilts, or if maybe they use boats in the city. My head is full of questions, but all the grown-ups are busy packing. *Only the important stuff*, they keep saying, and I wonder about that, too. Dishes are important, but so is music, and so are the rocks that line the windowsill, and every single book. I know all of that won't all fit, though, even in our station wagon with seats up front and seats in the middle and funny little seats that lift out of the floor in the back. There are all five of us and Robin and her two little daughters. All of us in the station wagon, all the way to Florida.

By the time we finally leave, I have one box of toys and books in the back, and one knapsack of books and stuffed animals in my lap. I have clothes mixed in the suitcases with everyone else's; there are three of them in a row back there. One box of dishes. One box of books. One box of food. One box of last-minute treasures saved from the pile on the curb. The pile that kept growing as our big station wagon seemed smaller and smaller. We only ever had what we needed, but *need* is a word that changes to fit the moment, Mama says. Two adults and one kid in the front. One adult and two kids and two car seats in the back. Four windows we can still see out of. Two thousand and twenty-eight miles. Two long days. Eight cold meals. Twenty rest stops. Five naps plus fitful sleep under dark skies streaked with streetlights. Ten tantrums, only one of them mine.

We have somewhere to land, thanks to the network of Premies my parents met following Guru Mahara-ji. He's not one of those preachers who bounce up and down and talk about heathens when what they mean is people who aren't white or people who don't believe in god the right way. He has a round, brown face and a sleepy smile and teaches about knowledge and meditation and breathing and letting go of ego. It feels like the opposite of how angry religion usually is. There are gentle chanting songs

and ghee candles and potlucks and lots of laughter. Once, we go to a weekend festival where there's every kind of arts and crafts and giant spools turned into tiny forts, and we sleep in a big orange tent that's easy to find. A family my parents met at that festival has an apartment in Gainesville, and they say we can stay with them until another one opens in their complex. I barely remember them and their two small boys, but we've lived with lots of people, so I'm not too worried. When we finally pull up into the parking lot, though, I realize how different this will be from any place we've lived before. Two stories of dingy brick stretch in every direction, roughly grouped around open spaces of dirt and scraggly grass.

We drag everything up the stairs at once, even though we're tired, because Ben says it's not a good idea to leave it in the car. I've never really worried about anybody stealing anything of ours before, but this place feels hungry. Like hungry that doesn't ever get fed right. Everything is shades of beige and slightly sticky or gritty or both. Susan helps my mom and Robin get pallets set up for all the kids in one room and for themselves in the living room, and then we all mumble our way through another round of sandwiches and fall asleep. The next day is a blur of school registration and food stamps office, and I still haven't seen any water, and the trees all seem to be just behind that next big building, and the air is wet and thick in my lungs. My school has a big library, but there are so many kids and nowhere to go that is quiet. Not at school, not at home, and definitely not in the courtyards where kids from the same buildings tend to group together and claim the closest one.

Sometimes they are related, sometimes just the same race, and they don't often mix like I'm used to. Most of the other white kids I've met here seem scary and hateful, saying ugly things in lazy voices like they don't even care. I avoid them and everyone else, mostly. I try to make friends with a couple of black girls in the next courtyard over my first week, but they toss me around with hard hands and angry words until I scramble away.

My mama says it probably wasn't just about me, and I could sort of tell that when it was happening, but I also know something about me touched off pain for them. That people who look like me hurt people who look like them. New hurt on top of old hurt until it's giant and deep, and I must have said something, did something, that was like a sharp edge. A finger in a bruise. The adults in my family are determined to do better, to speak up when people say ugly things around them, so I resolve that I will too. There is too much pain in the world; I need to help. I need to understand.

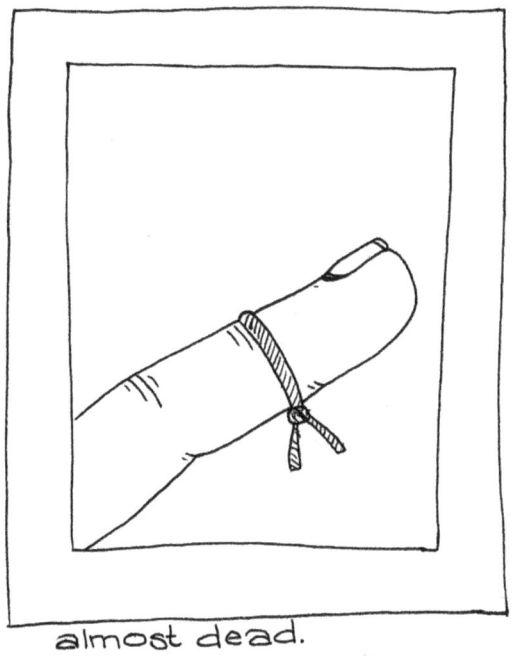

almost dead.

Pain is something I puzzle over a lot these days. Like when you wrap a string around the tip of your finger and it turns colors and loses feeling and then goes white and numb. Almost dead. Or how you can stitch a line through the top couple of layers of skin on your fingers and palm and hardly feel it at all. Or how, ever since that man (I don't remember) did that thing (I don't remember), I can't really feel any pleasure (I don't remember) when I touch myself, but there's nowhere private to be, and anyway, I have a new book to read. I grab a glass of water and a butter and sugar sandwich and tuck away into the spot behind the couch I found where the light comes in slanted and nothing can get behind me and I can't be seen. This other story, it's much better.

# Mama makes adventures / Daddy has magic eyes

Mama makes adventures with a left-hand turn and five dollars' worth of gas. She can find free ballet, hidden parks, and ducks who will be your best friend for three bites of stale bread. Museum exhibits, steel drums, garage sale treasure hunts. A clean house and a day off means piling into the car with a picnic of leftovers and no map at all. Laughter deep into your belly. Faces tired from wonder.

Daddy has magic eyes. One hazel, one brown. A little more almond, a little more round. We're at the stoplight, waiting for him to change it from red to green. "Not yet," he says. "Almost!" And we're watching him, watching the light, both odd eyes intent, and he finally starts to count – "Three, two, one, now!" – and the light turns green, and we cheer while he pulls slowly, carefully into the intersection and makes the turn.

Mama takes us on a long drive into the woods and out and around the lake and back into the woods, and it's late, almost bedtime, and there's nothing but treescapes and stars out the window. The sound of frogs, barely, then louder, then the car rolling to a stop while my youngest brother points and cries, "Oh, no!" The road is full of them, slow and glistening in the drizzle and the headlights. We sit there for half an hour, entranced past hunger, until they have all made the trip across the pavement into dark safety.

Daddy says a witch cursed his mom after being turned away at the door late one night. That his eyes are a side effect. That it gives him small powers, easy magic. Like the stoplights or the way he can see so well in the dark. He sings just off key, always mixing words or skipping a verse, louder over our groans, until we give in and sing along about the bullfrog, the rose, the lumberjack. Silly songs, not from the radio, only ever in the car. All the way to the stoplight, magicked red to green.

# Mermaid practice

The very best thing about our house, besides the big climbing tree, is the public pool down the street. It's so close I can walk there with the little kids for swim class and nobody asks to be carried. Not even when we stop to play in the giant piles of soft dirt left when another housing project fell through, racing up and around and sliding down until we all need a long shower before we can get in the water.

Floating feels like privacy. With my ears underwater and my eyes closed against the sun, I can pretend the sounds around me are nature. That the waves bobbing me and pushing me toward the edge are from the moon, not a cannonball. That everything about me is light and easy and pleasurable.

I can't trust that silence for more than about five minutes, though, even if I don't get splashed or bumped into. There are too many things in my head that will start to holler if I let them, and besides, I love to swim. I am strong and graceful in the water, diving deep and skimming the bottom for long minutes. Handstands and spins and underwater loops, breathing out through my nose in a steady stream to keep the water from coming in.

All of this is fun, of course, but I am in training. I'm going to be a professional mermaid. In Florida, nobody laughs when I say that. It's serious business in Weeki Wachee, swimming serene and lovely in giant tanks, sipping oxygen behind the kelp and flipping jeweled tails. I could make good money and go to college and spend the whole day in the water. I do another lap with my legs held tightly together, concentrating on making a smooth wave from my hips to my toes.

## SOSSITY CHIRICUZIO

I practice smiling, eyes open, like I live underwater. Like I'm totally comfortable. The trick is to scull gently with my hands to hold my position halfway between the floor and the air for a long, slow moment then break the surface with a dramatic flourish. I always come home from the pool with sore, red eyes and wrinkled toes, tender from pushing off hard from the concrete bottom to get momentum for my twisting arch back into the water.

The only thing that fascinates me more than mermaids is ballerinas. My mom takes me to see every free show, and I study their movements, how they hover in the air but not like flying, it's like floating. All my organs shift upward for that impossibly long moment – my heart in my throat, my stomach banging around in my chest. The dancers land like dandelion seeds, twirling on that tiny point, joyful and vibrant, so easily it seems.

When my mom finds out the county is offering an after-school ballet class, I can't wait to sign up. I know it's a late start, but I study every move the teacher makes, holding tight to the barre while I try to find my center. Every class is hard but fun, and by the third one I feel like I'm finally starting to figure it out. When the teacher asks me to stay after, I think she's going to tell me she agrees, but that's not it. "I have to tell you…" she starts, and I suddenly feel ill. Her face is so carefully expressionless. "You can keep taking the class, of course, but you are just not built to be a ballerina."

I look down at the breasts that insist on growing, past my rounded tummy and down to my feet. The feet I was so carefully pointing just five minutes ago – first position, plié, second position, arms high, remember to smile, back to first – are now awkwardly shuffling. Too big, all of me, suddenly. I make myself look up at her, but she's looking at the wall somewhere over my head. She pats me stiffly on the shoulder and I shrink out from under her hand.

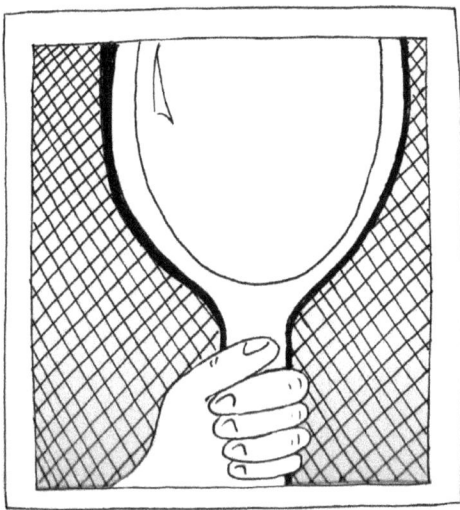

I feel the numbness spreading from that point of contact, across my shoulder blades, down into my hips, down my legs, my arms. Everything getting stiff and distant again.

When I get home I pull out the beautiful picture book of *Swan Lake* my mom got me for my birthday last year and go slowly through the pages. Looking carefully at the bodies. Everything long and slender. Barely any curves, nothing out of place. Sleek and controlled, precise and sharp. I get the mermaid coloring book off my sister's shelf and look closely. The water seems to be more forgiving – arms and hair loosely waving, hips curving into the muscle of the tail, but still. Slender. Sleek. Long.

I put the books away and look in the mirror. Roundness, everywhere. My cheeks, arms, belly. Short legs, a crooked tooth in my smile. Hair that is often unruly. I feel the numbness lay down another layer of white noise, buzzing against my memories of the building symphony of sound, of the rush of bubbles against my skin. I will never twirl on my toes, never flip my tail and smile.

# Three in the hand

They are tiny miracles and sometimes also a whirling dervish of emotions. They are tender and joyous. They are work. They are play. There had only ever been grown-ups before, holding me tenderly. There had only ever been me trying to understand. Now, I'm finding solutions and bandaging knees. Now, I'm responsible.

It's terrifying, in moments. They cry and sometimes bleed. They could die. They ask questions I'm unsure of or am still struggling with myself. They remain stubbornly individual. Which I love, but not always. They look right at me and still love me. They are sometimes afraid for me, but I vow they'll never be afraid of me.

My wild-haired flower. My dark-eyed watcher. My sunshine and shadows.

I know by now of the dangers in the world, the ones we hear about and the ones that almost everyone hides. I know I can't possibly save them from everything, but I'm determined to try. I back off school bullies, a stray Doberman, and even the predator across the street, once I'm sure that's his game. Small victories, but lacking a sword, I make use of the shield at hand.

Small protections, tuna noodle casserole served in absolute portion fairness, bedtime stories. Managed chaos. Not hero stuff, just helping. Just family, working together. Just beyond my reach sometimes, but we survive. Play pretend for long hours, keep the house reasonably clean and don't burn it down.

Once in a while a fight, followed by sorrow and hugs. Once in a while a moment alone.

# Poetry and puberty

As if it weren't enough, to be so different. As if I didn't already stand out like a target. Over the summer I got my period, grew breasts, grew them larger. Too big for the training bras or any of my favorite shirts. Or seventh grade. Too big for my skin, already marked with shiny trails like the ones on Mama's belly. Heavy. Dangerous.

The boys are talking about them, the crudest words, the whispers, sharp like broken fingernails, while I stretch out my T-shirt every chance I get, hoping for loose, for hidden. Other girls kissing boys in the hallways, other girls holding hands with them, but I'm the bad girl. Scared of touching anyone, yet I have the reputation. I'm hiding and crying in the bathroom, trying to put in a tampon, and the applicator is awkward and hard edged, and I can hear them talking outside the stall.

The boy they say got to third base with me has never touched me, though I had admired the sun on his hair. He stopped by my house one afternoon, lounging against the porch and saying almost nothing, eyes measuring me, and away, and again. He left after less than an hour. I just stood by the door, arms crossed and elbows cupped, watching the kids in the yard. It seemed like I should feel something, but it was all a mystery. Not one I wanted to solve. Just some boy I didn't know.

If I am going to kiss a boy, it will probably be Ralph, I guess. Mass of curls and thick glasses, big books and D&D and Star Wars. It's not that I want to kiss him, but he seems like the best option, if I have to kiss a boy. He invited me to the movies last week; *Xanadu* just came out, and I love Olivia Newton-John, or maybe I want to be her. I asked my parents, and my dad took us and then sat between us. I was a bit embarrassed but also relieved. Ralph didn't seem particularly upset either, and next week we did geography homework like usual.

Loretta also has soft curls and glasses, a subtle humor and a watching nature that I like. We go roller-skating sometimes and watch movies, read books, talk about nothing much. I want to ask her what it's like for her, does she walk through the world on alert? Is she afraid? Is she happy? I think these are unusual questions, or at least, nobody else seems to ask them. I think all girls must be afraid. I think maybe none of us have the words.

English is my favorite class, and our teacher this year is younger, more alive, looks right at us. She always does something interesting, but today was more. Today was answers and better questions. Today was poetry! She passed out these packets of paper but told us not to open them yet. Told us to close our eyes and just listen. The music was full of violin and odd electronic notes and words that didn't tell a story. They told the idea of a story, a story pulled open into words and spaces with room for my own thoughts.

When it was done, she told us to open the packet to the first page, and there were the words, bare of music, just my eyes to read them, my mind to hold them. No rhyming, no syllables hammered into a structure, just images lit up like neon, like sunrise, like cartoon dreamworld gone solid. Stories without endings. Sadness without explanation. Joy like a bouquet. Words that color other words, that nest inside them, that need reading twice. Three times.

A voice for fear. For anger. For love. For confusion. A voice for not hiding. A voice for sunlight. For rainstorm. A voice to ride over the other voices with courage, with head-high, banner-waving truth. For tiny-tender-in-my-curled-hand truth that I don't have to show anyone. For connecting. For privacy. A voice I can plant my story in, to show and to not show. A voice for mystery. A voice for knowing. For freedom.

# Summertime

Blue jug, deeper than I'd ever want to go. Ichetucknee River, otters tumbling alongside and water bubbling like crystal balls. Up from the white sand whipping past our feet. Rubber warm in the sun and hugging us safely afloat. Cold so that only summer heat will suffice.

Swimming with the alligators in Lake Wauburg, always watching for the bumpy, lumpy log that could be hungry. Only up to our waists, close enough to run for the shore. Hot dogs sizzling loud. Baby oil spread across shoulders and legs baking quietly into leather.

Bluegrass and belly-flop contests, rocking the surface until the watermelons and six-packs dance. Shocking pink and freezing cold. The slice of melon, the redneck stomach. Great arches of green, pools of shadow and blue flag iris. A landscape I wish I could disappear, tiny, into.

# The house that crumbled

All buildings in Florida have bugs, no matter how much you clean. They were the worst part of the projects, and my skin still crawls thinking about the sound they made. You have to turn the light on around the corner and wait for the flood to recede before entering a room. They spray the buildings one at a time, and the roaches just retreat to the next building and the next. A horrible game of hide-and-seek where the bugs always win.

Our new house mostly doesn't have bugs inside, but it's built up over a crawl space that is hidden behind cracked wooden lattices. Just about anything could be under there. Living under the floor, under our beds, under our feet. I don't think about it very often, until the hole in the bathroom floor. It doesn't start off as a hole, just tiny ripples in the linoleum. It was clean and new and smooth when we moved in, but after a few years, it starts to peel up around the edges, and there is a spot between the toilet and the tub that feels mushy under the tile. It eventually erodes away, and then the hole starts to grow.

At first, it's the size of a pencil, standing on end. In fact, my brothers drop a couple down one afternoon before I catch them, the good pencils with plenty of eraser left. I cajole my brothers outside with promises of a game of horses, but the hole keeps growing, slowly, when we're not looking. Then it's the size of a quarter, and sometimes it catches our toes and trips us. We try not to step on it, but the bathroom is small, and there are six of us, and the hole keeps growing until it's the size of a closed hand and then an open one.

Now it grows faster, like it's got the hang of it, and you can see the crawl space underneath. It's not just about bugs or snakes or even falling through. The bathroom is the only private place – if nobody breaks in with a straightened-out wire hanger through the hole in the knob. What if the floor gives way when I'm in the bath and the whole tub falls into the crawl space and I'm naked and covered in bugs and the firemen have to pull me out? What if it happens when my parents aren't home and the kids get scared and forget how to call for help? What if I have to crawl through the dark and the bugs and break through the lattice and then I'm naked outside?

I remember when I was younger and naked was fun. When it was sunshine and breezes and easy. Now, it's nightmares where I fall through the floor or I forget to get dressed and start walking to school and don't realize it until I'm halfway there, and all the men can see me and there is nowhere to hide. I remember when I was little, before any of the other kids were born, and we all went swimming naked. My mom, my dad, their friends, and it wasn't weird or scary. It was just skin and smiles and water and shapes. Now, I wear a swimsuit and a T-shirt, and I still feel exposed.

I feel the safest out back, up a tree. We have our own tiny forest, with tall, skinny pines and a wide, spread magnolia and my favorite, the gumbo limbo tree. It's perfect for climbing, with sturdy branches that are easy to grab and deep forks to snug into with a book or just to watch the sky. There are a few branches low enough for the kids to play on without getting hurt, but the top of the tree is my own special place. I can see everything around me and people almost never look up.

There are clotheslines strung between some of the pines, sometimes parades of underwear and socks, sometimes flapping flags of sheets. Dad tried to ride the new motorcycle between two of the pines and bent both handles and bruised every knuckle. He was trying to show Mama that he knew how to ride. That it was a good thing that he sold our second car that could at least carry some kids and groceries and bought this instead. We'll save so much on gas, he said. I totally know what I'm doing, he said. She got really quiet, like she does before she gets really loud, and then, BAM! He ran into the trees.

You can't see any marks on the trees, and after a few months, you can't see any marks on his hands, either, but the motorcycle is gone the next morning. They don't talk about it. There are more silences these days. More swing shifts and fewer gatherings. More stress lines and less laughter. Even a house with a hole in the floor costs money, and they both work so hard. I'm starting high school soon and will get home from school later, which means figuring out childcare, and we don't seem to have as much community as we used to. More Little League and fewer potlucks. I can't remember the last time I saw anyone meditating.

Mama gets a good deal on a pair of white four-poster beds from one of the rich houses she cleans on the weekends, and my sister is excited about the Holly Hobby canopy that comes with her bed, but I string sheets like curtains from post to post on mine. I can still hear everything though, it's not private, so I push all my clothes over to the side in my closet and make a little nook with pillows and a flashlight. I make a sign with my name on it in my most careful cursive, cutting it out of thick cardboard into a cloud shape and tacking it to the door. "Don't come in!" I say, as if anyone else would fit. All I want these days is to be alone. To breathe air that didn't just come out of someone else's mouth and to hear the sound of my heartbeat in my ears. To be singular.

I love my siblings, even when they make me feel crazy, even when they are loud and touch my stuff and won't do their chores. Mostly we have fun and laugh, but right now, I just want time to figure out who I am. Time to think slow thoughts and wander through the house without looking for anybody or their shoe or their keys. I start high school, and there's even more people – 3,000 students, all of them seeming to understand how it works better than me. I'm excited about the advanced Earth Space science class and art and weight training, but I'm surrounded all the time. I don't know what to do with these feelings or myself. I feel prickly under my skin and my tongue is sharp. There's a tension in the house I can't quite figure out, and the hole in the bathroom keeps getting closer to the tub and the toilet. Now we have to watch where we put our feet all the time.

Mama finally comes to me and says we're moving. Back to Arizona. That Grannie has a house we can stay in while we look for our own place and that I'll be going to high school in Tombstone, as in Wyatt Earp and the Wild West, and I don't know what to say. I barely have any friends to leave, but at least some faces are starting to look familiar. She says it will be another adventure, but her eyes are tired and sad. Change is hard, but the ground doesn't really feel steady here anymore. Dad and my sister leave early so he can start working and she can start school, and now it's a flurry of packing and last visits with everyone and hardly a moment to climb a tree. This house we owned, the only one ever that was just ours, came from a VA loan, which I know means because my dad fought in a war, but now we're leaving and still broke and somehow it doesn't belong to us.

Everything is packed, just the cleaning to do, and we save the bathroom for last. After we've taken turns washing our hands, Mama leaves to go through the house one last time for anything

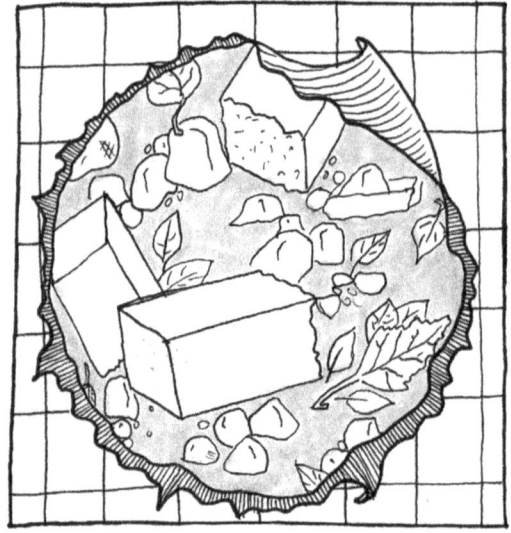

forgotten. I look down into the hole for several long moments, and eventually my eyes adjust and the underneath is dim, not pitch-black. Broken bricks, dead leaves, lots of dust. Nothing moving, or if it is, it's something small. I can even see the streaks of light from the far wall through the lattice. Scary, but not the worst thing that could happen.

# First day

The bus stop is a shallow pull out on a long stretch of back road. There're five or six of us standing in small, strung-out clumps in the red dust, while the desert and the sky stretch out around us so far it makes me dizzy, just a little. I'm looking at the other kids, trying to get a sense of what I'm in for, and this one girl is polished like nothing I've ever been close to. Everything just so and matching and brand-new, hair smooth as running water past the diamond flashes in her ears. She catches my eye and cuttingly asks if I have a staring problem, and the other kids are edging in, or away, and the long empty road and I have no idea where I am and I shrink into myself, staring down while they are all laughing for the endless ten minutes until the bus finally shows.

Forty-five minutes later, we get off the bus, and I've already got a nickname. *Weirdo.* She sweeps past me, bumping shoulders, trailed by a horde of similarly polished girls, and I don't want to go in there, and I don't have a choice, and this giant yellow bleach stain on the back of my puffy green jacket feels like a target, or maybe it's just me. The front office is the usual hassle of spelling my name, and again, and pronouncing it, and again, and they still look at me oddly. Finally the paperwork is done, but somehow there is no locker so I'm carrying seven books and a stomach made of lead down these hallways full of black-and-white senior class photos all the way back to 1922 and kids right now and everyone is a stranger.

First period is biology, which is fine, and the teacher is quirky, which is better, and I get through it and slide, relieved, into my seat in English, trusting my way with words and hoping we'll get to read something, anything, just for a respite. I grit my teeth through algebra and PE and then look for the cafeteria. There isn't one. The office worker tells me free lunch is served at the elementary school, about eight blocks away, and hands me a Xeroxed map. I take my pile of books out and down the street until I find a boulder behind a wall and set it all down and hug that warm, solid surface to me like armor, blocking out the light and the thoughts and the rumble in my stomach. It only lasts until the bell rings.

The rest of the day starts to blur, and I'm just watching the clock face and trying to breathe until the big noisy rush to the buses, and I'm swept along and up the steps, and then people are pushing past me because where will I sit? I finally find someone who doesn't stare past me or at the ground, and I scrunch down, hoping for invisible. There's shuffling behind me, whispering, movement. Laughter, but sharp edged. The silence is spreading out until the only sounds are right behind me, and then splash and thud, thick liquid and solid lumps slapping onto the top of my head, slopping down onto my shirt, and the smell is soda and tobacco and candy and spit and bubblegum, and I'm standing up somehow, staring all around me, and everyone is a stranger.

Nobody offers a seat or a handkerchief. There are pockets of cackling raucous laughter, and smaller ones of shamed or fearful silence. The hierarchy is clear, and I am marked outcast and weirdo and trash. I am dripping onto the floor of the aisle and we are fifteen minutes out of town and too far to turn back. I make my way to the steps next to the driver, who gives me a sympathetic look but is obviously not taking on the system for me. I sit, feeling the disgust harden in my hair and wish with every last shred of childish belief for this all to be a bad dream, but I know it's not. I'll have to survive tomorrow, too.

# We need the dream

Ruth and I both love horses, wear jeans and plaid shirts, are strong and kind of skittish around boys. We live in remote parts of the desert, where going anywhere means miles of walking or begging a ride. We are both dirt poor. No shiny new shoes. No hamburger lunches with straw wrappers and easy laughter flying. Free lunch program and the outside edge of a bus seat, grudgingly given. Home-cut hair and hand-me-downs. These rare afternoons of horse care and trail rides and Uno are an escape for us both. Not only from boredom and chores but of the need to hide our empty pockets.

## SOSSITY CHIRICUZIO

I will sometimes, but not often, stay the night. The horse corral, her room – these are good places. Full of comfort and easy conversation. Her father, however, poisons every moment he is a part of. His is a sneaky cruelty meant to shame. Anything she values is fair game. Any audience who cares makes it better for him, especially if it is another teenage girl. I never let him within four feet of me, wear my baggiest clothes and stare hate at him. I wish I could make him disappear for her, don't even try to disguise it.

Her horse is everything to her. Riding, grooming, training him to barrels, feeling that freedom of movement. She has been carefully growing out and tending his mane and tail for months, getting ready for the rodeo, hoarding change for ribbons and practicing plaits. Every bit of pride her life doesn't allow for her own sturdy beauty is poured into that chestnut coat, that black horsehair. One afternoon just three days before show time, her father saunters into the house, swinging a large, rusty pair of shears. "Spring haircut..." he drawls, and she's already out the door, running for the stable.

I find her swallowing rage and tears, face pressed hard against that broad shoulder while all around their feet lie ragged hanks of hair. Cut right down to the bone of the tail, and in inch-long clumps along his neck, unrepairable. Unbearable. Had he come out to view the effect of his deed, he might've found how dangerous two downtrodden horse-crazy teenage girls could be with a pitchfork. With some predator's sense of danger, he chooses instead to head to the bar to laugh about how sensitive womenfolk are.

I stay all day, through endless games of cards, and distract her with fantasies about a horse ranch run only by women.

As usual, ramen is the only food available, and not the freshest ramen at that. As we carefully strain the weevils out with the water, mutually ignoring the fact of what we are doing with practiced moves, the dream of owning land stands stark in my mind as impossible. As with the weevils, we ignore it. We need the dream.

# Monsoon

The stars seem closer than usual, even accounting for the fact that I'm up a tree. The storm pushes them toward me or me to them. The leaves flatten against the wind, dream of flying free. Or maybe that's me again.

The lightning stretches blue-white light across the length of time-worn mountains and the backs of my eyelids. My skin is tingling from widow's peak to toes curled tight against peeling bark.

I'm snugged into a thick crook, hugging the trunk, head back and mouth open to better taste the ozone. To better smell the creosote, wet for thunder. Want is deep in me like a jagged splinter, invisible pressure on a bundle of nerves, impossible to grasp with my fingers.

Almost all I've known of sex is pain. Passive and stolen away. This rough tumbling of air and electricity, this press of sap and breath and gravity, is another channel entirely. I want to open up like roots to water. Want to climb the sky.

# Shoulder to shoulder

His skin is dusty black from dashing through the desert to catch the bus. Always almost too late, laughing between gulps of air. Falling into the bench seat at the back with the rest of us bad kids. Falling against me, but not like an attack. Like belonging. He talks me out of a handful of my popcorn then gives most of it back. Face twisted up at the taste of nutritional yeast. Stick and poke tattoos on his forearm flashing as he reaches past me to slap his friends into wrestling.

"Draw this for me," he says in art class. "You're so much better at it." I try to convince him to follow my example, to pick up the ideas of shape and space, but I finally realize his art form is convincing me. Survival skill plus natural charm. A test without malice, a figuring out of me. I banter like a girl and lift weights like the only girl in the gym. One that can keep up, even lift more than some of them. Lift some of them. Smart and not afraid to show it. Afraid all the time but not showing it.

He sees me, actually pays attention enough to notice when I pull away or shut down. He's not at all sure what to do about it, but it's enough that he sees. That he respects. Unlike the others, so I begin to trust him. Share truths along with the joints, talk about writing, about leaving. He talks about music, drumming like a superpower. Like it could set him free. We exchange thrashing heavy metal and old-school rock tapes, blast Violent Femmes like a battle cry, cut creative holes in our band T-shirts.

## SOSSITY CHIRICUZIO

End of the day, same bus, same seat, his eyes measuring my response. There is a pull between us. He thinks maybe it means we should lie down, but I know we belong shoulder to shoulder. I also know I don't want to stop liking him, which is where lying down leads. Better to arm-wrestle or make a mosh pit. Slap down the bones in mathematics of five. Aim our voices at the sky. We're both bundles of nerves under nervous skin, out of place in this quiet little town. We're both lost, but not with each other.

# Tired of have not

I was raised with a strong sense of justice and fairness among people who share easily and often. Nobody has much, but nobody goes without. There are plenty of toys, of books, of clothes, none of it new but no less good for that. Until public school. Until the contests of popular began and secondhand was second class. I hold firm against the taunting until high school, when every day is a war. Everything about me is a target. My name, body, brain, all counting against me. I am tired. Tired of have not. Tired of making do.

I don't remember the first thing I stole, but I remember whole lists of things I didn't. Things I never had. I have my own rules – no stealing from people or small businesses or just for fun. I know it doesn't make it OK, but it makes it bearable. Most of what I steal I give away. None of my friends have much either, and whether it is caretaker or courtship, I want something to offer. That giving streak, it runs in the family, and I'm not the first to make questionable choices in service of it.

I swipe steel-tipped three-inch heels from a factory discount store on a trip up to Tucson. Slip my fingers in the toes on my way past the table and out the door, so smooth my friend walking next to me doesn't notice a thing. I wait until we are in the car to tell her, knowing she'll freak out. Knowing also that she enjoys living vicariously through me and my bad girl ways. Knowing these shoes hold some fundamental piece of my forming identity that makes them a need, not just a want.

## SOSSITY CHIRICUZIO

I wear them with tight skirts and silky blouses and a black cotton duster, wide-brimmed Aussie hat on my head and dark sunglasses. I learn how to walk in them quickly, climbing the stairs to collect the slips that show who is missing from class, and turning (most of) them in. Working in the front office gives me freedom to prowl the halls alone and give my friends and other weirdos a break. Not always, but if they really need it. High school is a sequence of forced circumstances, and sometimes it's just too much. Sometimes the need to slip away and lick our wounds in private, or in drunken company, is too big. Those slips, they get lost on the way to the office. Sometimes.

I steal bras and underwear, makeup and seven silver rings of varying designs that I give to the group of girls I most often hang out with. Misfits and nerds and poor kids, a Venn diagram of different that gives us safe ground to meet on. It is 1988 and none of us has found the language of feminism to hang our thoughts on, but we stand strong together. Spin stories of protection and revenge against men who hurt us or want to. Support one another's crushes, even if we share them. Pass notes and make up code names, quirky semi-precious stones. I have no words for the safety net they give me, the hope they embody. I want to give them a token of gratitude, and my clever fingers slip seven shiny sparks of love into my pocket.

# My high school sweetheart

He is kind, really. One of the only teenage boys I've ever known who isn't looking to get something from me. Well, other than a friend and some kind of cover. I figure that part out later. If I am his alibi, though, he is also mine. Ash is tall and well built, smart, and talks to me like a person with a brain. My first day of school, he finds me wandering and lonesome, carrying all my textbooks and a fair amount of shame. He takes half of them from me and shows me around.

He is the only guy in the group of girls that forms over the next couple of years. They all find him dreamy but distant

and envy me for having such a hold on him. Not that we are ever super specific about it, but it is clear to anyone who wonders that we are a couple. Or something. Never seems to keep people from calling me a dyke when insults are flung. I imagine it doesn't always save him from being called faggot, either. But my hickeys are genuine, if a bit routine, and after we clumsily make out a bit we always find interesting things to do like archery or exploring the ravines or riverbanks behind his house.

Ash takes me to a family gathering in Tucson once. Big, interesting crowd in a big, interesting house, and everybody is really nice. At dusk, we take a walk with some of his younger cousins out into the washes, where we're talking about old rock and whether anyone can make a band like Led Zeppelin these days. The awe of the younger folks, the dim lighting, and the reflected courage from Ash sweeps me away, and I stand in the sand and the shadows and sing "Stairway to Heaven," a capella. I feel mysterious and strong for a full five minutes, and everyone is quiet, listening. He takes my hand when we walk home. I feel seen. Simple contact, such a difference, such a relief.

He introduces me to weed, classic Tombstone style. We find a soda can and slip away to the courthouse. Not the one they actually use, but the one just off the boardwalk, where you can view relics of people's lives and reenact a trial for social studies class. There's a giant sphere of a safe outside, in a small concrete enclosure, open to the sky. You can tuck right in behind the safe and not be seen, while the smoke drifts up and away. He carefully bends the can in the center and makes a shallow depression, then borrows my red mesh earring to punch a series of holes. The trick is to make the hollow deep enough that the wind doesn't blow the weed away into the dust, where you'll never, ever find it. I cough a few times, of course, but catch on quick.

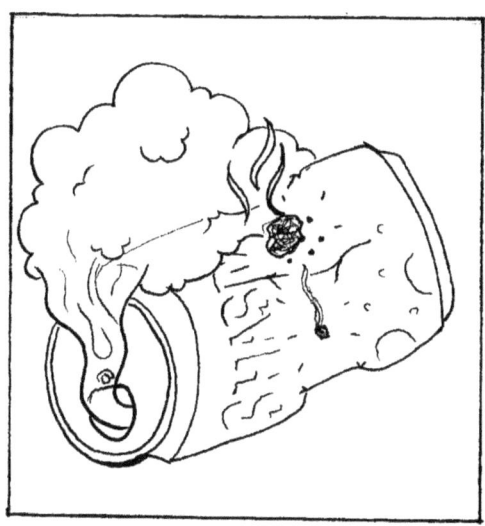

I love the soft buffer of weed and feeling happier, and almost comfortable in my own skin.

We have sex once. He is my first, if you don't count any of the violations of my childhood, and I try really hard not to. We agree that we are the right ones to lose our virginity with, and that we trust and love each other. It is awkward and painful and quick, neither of us moved by desire, just a need to have done it. To be able to say we had done it. Who's going to ask, we aren't sure, but being virgins is definitely a liability, especially since we are both trying so hard to be read as straight. Not that we discuss that part. He is gentle afterward, bringing me aspirin and holding me. We agree that we never need to do that again and go back to the way we were before, topic closed.

He finally cuts and runs, dropping out of high school and leaving for California when he can't squash himself into a tiny box anymore. A few experiments with guys on the army base make it clear to him, and he chooses truth. I love him all the more for it, even though it leaves me adrift in my junior year. He comes back to take me to prom, like he promised, though it turns out he has tickets to the U2 concert in Tucson that weekend and maybe I'd like to go to that instead? His uncle is driving up in his van and will give us a ride and a place to crash. Of course I say yes, and my mother helps me pack and doesn't tell me that she has a prime ticket to that show herself. She just smiles and sends me out on an adventure and gives hers away.

We sit in beanbags in the back of the van, sorting out all the seeds and stems from our bag of cheap weed and drinking black velvet from a bota bag. I feel like the friendly ghosts of my parents' past are along for the ride in a ritual-with-your-ancestors kind of way, and I heft the bag to the sky before shooting that clear stream down the back of my throat. Once we get to the theater, we find that we have nosebleed seats but feel so worldly and defiant we don't even care. Away from everyone who knows us, away from the familiar landscape and narrow horizon. The music is loud, it pushes right into our brains, seeps all the way into our fractured hearts. We sing along until we lose our voices and then sleep on the fold-out couch that night, cuddled for comfort and easy in our friendship. He knows who he is, and I am beginning to understand myself. It is plenty.

# Rite of passage

By my senior year of high school, I know I'm not straight, even though I don't know that word yet. I just know I'm not what everyone around me seems to be. I'm not sure I'm done with men, though every time I have sex with one I like them and myself less.

I remember my first love, Samantha, she of the red hair and impish smile. We did everything together the summer I was five, nothing coerced or inappropriate, just healthy curiosity and genuine affection. I learned about pleasure with her first, and also courage. She could pee standing up, challenged the boys at their own games, was sturdy and unafraid. Looking back, that childhood summer was the only point of light in the murky starfield of sex, and it was far and faint on the horizon.

Until I was six, men were just another kind of person. They taught me about the different strokes you can use with crayons and pens to make more interesting shapes when you color. They taught me that massage is about seeing with your fingers and finding the sore spot and helping it calm down. They taught me about music and bicycles and cooking and meditation. They had long hair and gentle hands. They were young but seeking wisdom. They carried me, hugged me, brushed my hair, tucked me in. They were safe.

There was no reason for my mother to balk at my spending time alone with any of them. We were a community. Collective childcare and potlucks and heart-wide-open connections. Trust. What kind of grown-up has sex with a child?

What kind of grown-up would even consider it? The human kind. The broken kind. The hurt-when-they-were-children-too kind. Believe me, I know all the reasons. I can even sort of forgive, in a theoretical way. Out of pity. But I can't do it out of love.

I don't remember his name. I remember blond hair and a beard. I remember buttons on a vest. I remember his cutoff denim shorts, and when I realized he wasn't wearing underwear. It was the first time I ever felt weird about a human body. Nudity was not a big deal in our community; I'd definitely seen a penis before. But I'd never had one displayed to me.

We lived in a big community house across the street from some row apartments, most of them rented by people we knew. The courtyard in front of them had a sprinkler system, pretty rare in Phoenix, and as usual, it was really hot. I was the only kid in our group who wasn't a baby, and I was used to playing by myself and in the company of adults. After the sprinklers shut off, I was hungry, and he offered me some lunch. He made spaghetti noodles with butter and Parmesan. Very common kid meal, very comfort food. Something I still eat on occasion, though I wonder at being able to stomach it.

Afterward, he said I should shower, which seemed odd, but I was kind of sticky from playing in the dusty grass. He came in to start the water for me, and then didn't leave. By the time I realized it, he was already naked and in the stall with me. He towered over me, like the tile walls, like the showerhead. I was cornered and too shocked to move. He laughed and talked like nothing strange was happening. Like he wasn't soaping up and exploring every part of my tiny body. Like he wasn't knocking his erection against my back and cheeks. Like this wasn't happening. But it was.

I should've screamed, should've run, should've fought. That lie every survivor is supposed to beat themselves up with is apparently bundled in with the abuse. What actually happened was my first experience of disassociation. I lay on my back, staring at his spray-textured ceiling, and tried to ignore the bizarre fact of his face between my legs. There were twitches of pleasure, because nerve endings don't always stop sending signals even when you don't consent. It felt like not only him but my own body was betraying me. He eventually stopped and immediately went to wash his face. Like it was dirty, or I was. I certainly felt gross, didn't want to feel the touch of my own skin. So I sank below it another inch or two while he handed me my clothes and explained how this was our secret.

Did he threaten me? Did he threaten my family? I can't remember what he said, or why I let it stop me from asking for help. I knew I could tell my mother anything, knew that she'd always protect me. I still can't explain why I didn't, why he was able to catch me alone at least two more times after that, or when he moved away. There's a rather big gap in my childhood memories after that. I know that shrimp, which used to be a favorite, made me gag from then on. Something about the texture reminds me of a forced mouthful of him.

When I was old enough to understand how babies were made but didn't have all the fine details, I worried for a full week that maybe his sperm were still alive, swimming around inside me, and that when I started my period, I'd get pregnant. It took quite a few indirect questions and some serious researching in the public library to put my mind at ease. I was teeth-gritting glad to know that at least some part of him had died.

# If I remembered their names

Neighbor boy spying on me in the bathroom, chasing me farther into the empty house. Cornering me in his bedroom. Tripping him to get away, wishing I could hurt him more. Being force fed rage.

The man who flashes me in the car, broad daylight, baby brother in his car seat next to me doing his puzzle. Not seeing. Not understanding my tears. Numb and cold in the bright sun, afraid it's me, that I'm a magnet somehow. Afraid for my sister, my brothers, afraid all the time.

The creepy man in the trailer park across the way tries to trick me and my siblings into being touched. I can't save myself, but I won't let them be hurt too. I tell my mom, she calls the police, a case is brought, they put little kids on the stand and then call them liars. He walks free. I learn the lesson. The system is broken, or people are, and justice is just a word.

When we move back to Arizona about six weeks into my freshman year, I have a chance to start over. I bury myself in my books and big baggy shirts and my safe relationship with Ash. Once he leaves, I decide to avoid sex until I can find someone I actually want. I have more than an inkling it will be another girl but no expectation of finding her where I am. Tiny, backward high school in a tiny, backward town. Already suspected of being gay, already suspect in every way.

I have never been to a real party before, but a girl in my neighborhood who sometimes talks to me has a bunch of people over one night when her mom is out of town and invites me. I imagine she thinks she is doing me a favor, and for the first forty-five minutes I think so too. A guy who graduated a year or two before is there, blowing off steam after a breakup. He sees me alone in the corner and brings me an open beer. I haven't really drunk much before, other than a bit of Boone Farm one night, which didn't hit me very hard.

I gulp the first half, trying to be cool. He stays with me far longer than I would've thought, and when I start to feel dizzy, helps me to the bathroom. Then he locks the door and starts to take off my clothes. I try to fight, or at least, in my head I do. My body is a rag doll. I have no idea what is happening, and I have no control over my limbs or voice. I'm watching and crying while he moves me around to suit him.

When people have been banging on the door for about twenty minutes, he dresses me enough to take me out in the back yard, people laughing and making crude jokes about our "date" and hogging the only bathroom. Once there, he starts all over again, a long hour of numb friction while I stare up at the cold and empty sky. He finally finishes and leaves me there, sprawled in a patio chair in the darkest corner of the yard.

When I eventually get control of my body again I can't bring myself to go back into the house. I climb the eight-foot chain-link fence and stumble home. The next morning on the school bus, I'm trying to hide my red eyes and the mass of hickies he left behind and someone makes a sniggering reference to how I'm acting like I was "raped" at the party last night, making it clear they think I'm just embarrassed to be such a slut. I feel myself give up. It is obviously going to happen no matter what I say, so maybe I should beat them to the punch and say yes.

A failure of a strategy, obviously. They still come and then leave, and I am still a series of holes with a passably pretty face.

I try to avoid sex with other high school students. I already know the cost and don't want the drama. So, their older brothers or cousins. Seniors from the other high school. Soldiers on the neighboring army base. I get a summer job at the Department for Economic Security working the counter for Unemployment – the jackpot of inappropriate men who are too old for me. Most of them see an easy score, but a few of them fall for me. It surprises me every time, that they think they could even know me well enough to love me. That I could ever love someone who did that to me. The very reason I try so hard to avoid the boys in high school who call themselves my friends but still try to get my shirt off if the opportunity presents itself.

Some of the guys I hang out with and I are all smoking pot one night when I excuse myself to use the bathroom. I come back quietly enough to catch them arguing among themselves. I can't quite hear them, but body language can speak volumes. I tell them loudly that I'm not planning on blowing any of them, so can we skip over that and get back to talking about the concert last weekend? They all look embarrassed, but none of them look as ashamed as they should. And these are ones I like well enough to call friends.

The last man I date, and the only one who actually qualifies for that descriptor – by which I mean meets my mother and is seen with me in public – is Jack Mormon. I am his last fling with sin before he commits himself to the Church so he can marry a proper woman. Someone to love and have children with. He tries to store up a lifetime of perversion to hold him over – spankings and sex toys and fucking in the park on the hood of his car.

All of it sounding really sexy but really more numb friction and a smile on my distant face.

He takes me places but not with pride in me. In the fact that he is fucking me, yes, but my value is definitely what I let him do, not who I am. His parting gift to me is a handful of STDs that he's been carrying and passes on when the condom breaks. My parting gift to him and whoever comes after me is making him watch the biopsy, my cervix projected on a TV screen, a foot across and bleeding. His face going white with what I hope is sorrow as well as shame. His name I remember.

# Red dust under my feet

I set my feet to the horizon and walk halfway there. Those ancient teeth of mountains, worn flat and grooved, are chewing quiet on the setting sun. More orange and pink than they could ever eat, and it's rich. Deep, thick layer on top of layer until my eyes are groaning and full.

The red dust is under my feet, like it knows where I'm going. Like it's been there before. Like I'm the mote of dust and it is the knowledge of ages. I know this is true. I know the enormous anger I carry is smaller still. In the face of the universe or even just this stretch of desert.

I try to stomp it out as I go. Down, down, out. Let it go. Let my breath carry out the sick feeling that lives in my gut. Let the mesquite in. Let the soft quail sounds in. Let a silence that holds the songs of bats in. I walk for hours, but the road always loops back around. Still me.

# Road trip

Tanya, Jimmy, and I are driving from Arizona to Florida and back again in this little four-door that offers not one comfortable position to sleep along the way. It's the summer after graduating high school, and we're off on a grand adventure, celebrating adulthood. Never mind the letter from my mother giving me permission since I'm not eighteen until November, safely tucked into my duffel. Never mind that we've got less than $800 between us, and we have not so much a plan as four places we're definitely stopping. Never mind, we're on our way, and we feel unstoppable, wild and free.

Three days in we're just hungry, grouchy, and tired of one another's company. We're inching our way through the snarls of cul-de-sacs and strip malls in a suburb of Kansas City (Missouri side), dreaming of a shower and a door that closes everyone out. Jimmy hasn't seen his dad in about three years and is nervous. Tanya is worried he still won't like her or won't let them sleep together. I'm realizing that I have no idea how I'm supposed to behave, but this isn't anything new for me. There's not a place in the world I feel certain of that these days.

Jimmy's dad is ex-military but only technically. The house is run like a barracks, and every tiny thing has rules. He hates our music and Jimmy's hair and that Tanya and Jimmy are still together. They met in Germany, on the army base both of their fathers were stationed at, and have been together since Tanya was sixteen and Jimmy was fifteen. They used to sneak out to metal concerts

on their dates and lost their virginity together in a train station. They are in love in a way that makes other people jealous. That I'm secretly in love with Tanya makes it a particularly bitter feeling. I love Jimmy like a brother and not just out of survival.

He's a charming, lanky clown of a southern boy, frequently abandoned and defiantly joyful, even when terrified. Our family, full of freaks and weirdos and love and conversations, is like a magnet to him, though he never can fully explain why. We fold him in with all the other foundlings and gentle him through lessons and love and homemade meals. The first time he saw me meditating, his first thought was witchcraft, and though he was right in some ways, I used other words to explain it. He loves me, even though every step I take into myself confounds him.

We all go out to a concert and try to score some weed – our mutual high of choice and almost impossible to find that entire trip.

Beer makes me queasy, and being drunk feels unsafe, but being sober is worse. I'm horny and lonesome and scared to come out, riding in the back seat all through the summer. No weed, no alcohol, almost late for the show, we get in line to see Poison, opening for David Lee Roth. As soon as we get inside, we start pushing to the front but quickly get separated. I can see Tanya happily headbanging in the square of Jimmy's arms, but I get caught between the barrel bellies of two giant men and spend several minutes struggling to breathe.

By the time I fight my way back out of the crowd, I'm overheated and dehydrated, just this side of hyperventilating, and disoriented. I'm also stone-cold sober, which makes the conversation I'm having with the security guard who finds me leaning on the water faucet a vexing loop for us both. He is using every trick he learned in training to try to coax the name of the drug I'm on out of me, and I don't have air enough to explain over the sounds of neon-green hair metal. He finally figures it out or runs out of patience and leaves me alone. I spend the next two hours watching the concert from the doorway. David Lee Roth goes through six bottles of whiskey, though half of those are poured on women in the front rows. They seem to enjoy it.

On to Alabama, where most of Jimmy's family lives, and where I keep my mouth firmly shut until we drive away. Every instinct I have says I'm in a dangerous place to share my thoughts, or even if I keep my mouth shut. We are there three days and I spend most of it with a woman who lives in the same housing development. Her name is Teresa, she is young and pregnant and lonely and beautiful, and I want so badly to save her. She has long, dark hair, a softly rounded body, and a very possessive husband. He dislikes me from the start, but since I am Jimmy's "cousin" and helping her out with housework, he allows that I can visit when he is at work. I spend every moment trying to ease her day or make her smile, even if it means going to the Piggly Wiggly with food stamps so she can cook him dinner. I think I'm bringing her some joy or at least a bit of respite. I have no idea what she thinks.

On the road to Florida, I eat a sandwich of questionable ham. Seems some melted ice water has seeped into the bag in the cooler, and chemical reactions begin while we drive. I'm lying down as best as a bucket bench will allow, staring out the moon roof and trying to do some breathing exercises to keep the nausea under control while Jimmy and Tanya sing along to Queen. It's just after dusk, the sky is indigo at the horizon and a field of stars above. The lightning bugs are out, zipping past the glass, slamming into it, making luminescent trails while the car turns into winding curve after curve.

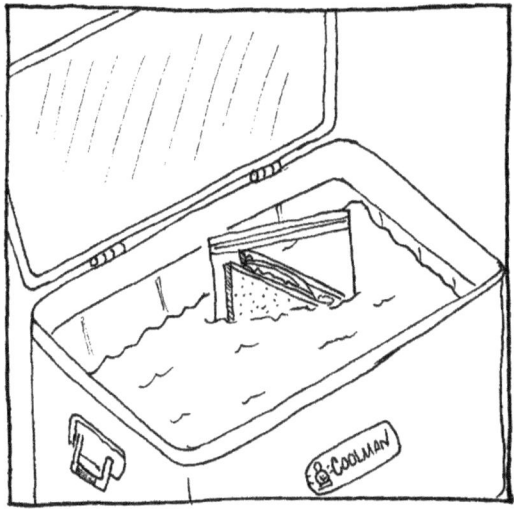

I realize the ache in my stomach is also lies and making do. I'm committed to this trip all the way to the Pensacola Bay and back; these two are my only safety net. My love for them feels a bit like a net too, and I'm starting to bleed through the empty spaces. I set my teeth against the wave of sick and dig my fingers in to ride it out.

# Gateway

The minute I get to community college, I start looking. Even though it is a tiny little campus in a tiny little city, there has to be someone like me there. There has to. I am losing hope and starting to feel like longing wrapped in skin, always thwarted.

Boys and men still approach me far more often than I want. I still tell myself it is a compliment. I don't want their attention, though. It's distracting. I am starting to truly admit to myself that I want a female lover. Want to explore that possibility, even if I'm not ready to use any of the words. Even if I'm not ready to examine the dissonance between wanting to have it and not wanting to be seen as it. I've been smacked around by those words too many times to feel eager to embrace them yet.

I am, however, eager to embrace Linda or Denise or both. It is confusing but exciting. They are both in my philosophy class and my tae kwon do class, and I can't stop watching them. They don't do anything obvious like hold hands, but they have a connection. I can feel it. They also arrive and leave together in a pickup truck, and they both wear wedding rings, but neither of them ever discusses a relationship or husband. They have the key or know where to find it. They have answers.

Denise is black, my height, curvy and sturdy in her slacks and blouses, with a wide smile, a sleek natural cut, and a husky voice. Linda is white, tall, lanky, and fairly androgynous in jeans and button-down shirts. Shoulder-length hair keeps her firmly in the female category, at least for the local barometer.

They are both strong-willed and smart and don't back down from the smarmy professor or the challenge of falling backward into a shoulder roll. I want what they have.

I hang out wherever they are, even if I have nothing to say. In fact, I'm frequently torn between wanting to say something clever so they'll know I'm smart and paying attention, and worrying that if I try, I'll completely fail. I feel so young and raw and unsure of myself. All the things men value me for, do they want that too? Do they care that I have big breasts? Is it all about oral sex? Would they want me if they knew how many men I've fucked? Would they want me at all?

I'm sitting behind Linda in class, carefully picking long hairs off the shoulder of her sweater. I tell myself it's allowable contact. I'm merely helping her keep that groomed look she seems to love. Ironed pleats, even in her jeans, with the cuffs just so across the top of her loafers. All the tiny touches of my fingertips to the nubby surface don't count. All the thoughts of what lies beneath – those are all secret. She doesn't even really see me; I'm just some new kid in the group. All through the class, one hair at a time, making it last.

What I don't know is the conversation that sparks with her and Denise. At first, they banter about how clueless straight girls are, all those overtures they can't even acknowledge. How they touch without thought, flirt without intent. As they talk, the examples of my attention become more obvious, start to form a picture. They realize that I'm not, perhaps, so clueless as they thought. That I might be reaching out, clumsy as it is. That I might be, as Denise says, a lost sheep.

The next day on campus, they are, as usual, sitting in a small group of interesting people. Everyone is talking politics and the upcoming election. I have so many feelings about it, want so badly to be one more vote against Bush, want so badly to participate. Despite this, I hope desperately that nobody will ask me who I will vote for. Not because I want to avoid the topic, but because of where that will lead. My eighteenth birthday is four days after the election. Incredibly frustrating, but also revealing far more than I want to. It's still a month away, which means I'm still a month from being of legal age. Still a kid, still not old enough to count.

I stand and casually gather up my things, hoping to make an unnoticeable exit, but Denise notices and puts her hand on my arm to stop me. I'm caught between elation (*She's touching me!*) and anxiety (*She won't want to touch me when she knows!*) and freeze in place.

"Who are you voting for?"

And there it is. A direct question I can't get around.

I look down and mumble, and she starts to lecture me about the importance of voting and being involved in the democratic process, but my expression makes her pause, and I blurt out, "I'm not voting! I want to! But I'm not eighteen until later in the month..." the last part in a trailing rush of words.

Denise and Linda look at each other, clearly surprised, and I can't stand to wait for what comes next. I pull free and rush off to find a corner of this tiny campus that feels less exposed. My face is burning, I'm fighting tears, and I just know I've blown it. They'll never let me in, and why would they? What could I possibly bring to the table? I don't know anything. I don't even know what I'm asking for. I tuck myself into a corner behind the art building and cry all through my next class, wishing someone would rescue me. Wishing I could rescue myself.

# Threshold

The elections come and go, disappointing, as is my birthday. I'm living in a trailer with some friends, in the desert outside town, no vehicle, no steady job, no real idea how to stitch it all together. However, I do have my own room for the first time in my life, and I'm legally an adult. To celebrate, I drop acid; I've never done it before. We watch *The Wall* and *George Carlin Live*, and I'm laughing and cuddled up against a friend, the gift of a bit of no-pressure physicality. I do have to occasionally flick beer out of my hair since we're all pretty loose with the details at this point, but whatever. Tanya and Jimmy slip off to their room, and I pretend not to care so well that nobody notices a thing. Every time she smiles at me with that soft touch of pity, I'm gratified and then angry, but mostly at myself. She's made it clear that though she tried sex with girls and it was fun, it's just not her thing. The fact that she hasn't told anyone about my confession of love but could makes my butterflies anxious and sharp-edged. I'm ready for someone I can love without apologizing. Someone I can love without fear.

After the humiliation of the election question incident, I stayed away for a week or so, but I'm slowly easing back into the conversations in the courtyard, trying to find some balance. Learning. Listening. I notice that Denise has a strong but subtle effect on the discussions, especially when someone starts to monopolize or grandstand. She draws out the quiet ones, reflects things beautiful and questionable back at their source, holds her ground. Gently. Like a boulder that is currently at rest is gentle. She keeps it moving forward, keeps it open. We turn to her for confirmations, for examples. She is a bright sun we are glad to orbit, while Linda zips through like a comet, brilliant bursts and long silences.

The contrast between my isolation in the trailer I share with Jimmy and Tanya and the bright afternoons of seeking and connection at school is stark. I've never had my own space, and I crave it every day. I find a tiny trailer in town so I can walk to school, find a job, close the door. The absolute luxury of room upon room with only myself. Door after door. Lock after lock, if I want. After a few weeks, I find locking the front door is enough, and sometimes sleep without a single nightmare. I hang my art. Cook my food. Read my books. Sing out loud.

Think about Denise and Linda.

Nothing about me wants to interfere with their relationship. They are happy, easy with each other. Beautiful. I can't stop thinking about them, and I can't imagine just one of them. It's bewildering, but insistent. I decide to make a gesture so obvious they couldn't miss it, even if they decide to ignore it. We have tae kwon do class tonight, and I am (almost)(mostly)(possibly) sure my plan is a good one. There is a tiny changing room for women, barely enough space for the five of us at the same time, so I feel justified in dawdling a bit until the three of us are the only ones in the room. I turn toward the lockers, take a deep breath, and slide off my tight jeans, revealing the bright-red, lacy G-string I chose this morning. All the rustling of clothing stops, for just a moment, then resumes. I finish changing into my dobok, tie on my yellow belt, and follow them into the dojo.

Have I gone too far? Are lesbians into lingerie? Did I insult them? Did they even see it as an advance? My mind is definitely not on the forms, and my cheeks are low-burning embers. Our teacher calls me to attention, and I force myself to focus, to move smoothly through the entire shape I trace out on the floor, arms just so. Feeling strong in my body, able to strike back, is important. As I sink into my mind and the patterns, I keep Denise and Linda in my peripheral, hoping for a long look, a smile. I catch them exchanging glances, and Denise has a quirk to her mouth, a raised eyebrow. I either chose well or won the award for being clueless.

After class, they invite me over. We eat something filling and simple, lined up on the couch in their living room. Their trailer is larger, nicer, filled with a shared life. Photos, albums, movies. We watch *Desert Hearts*, and my own races, ready to leap into any hand that is offered. They tuck me in on the couch and go down the hall to their room. I might cry but for the joy of knowing that a shared bed exists in this backward town, on this starry night. I dream of feasts and kissing and the ocean.

We spend several evenings like this over the next month while I continue to learn about gay films and women's music and the pattern of their lives together. Then, one Friday, they tell me that they have tickets to a reggae concert in Bisbee that night and invite me to join them. We get dressed at their place while they tell me the best ways of avoiding ID checks. I'm not worried as I haven't been ID'd since the first time I bought a gallon of wine and a fifth of Jack Daniel's at the corner store when I was seventeen. These tits are heavy but useful. We get into the bar just fine and split an eighth of shrooms. I hate the taste but soon forget it in the groove of music and the soft, sweet high spreading through me. Denise and Linda are somewhere in the crowd near me, but I dance solo, eyes closed and rapturous, spangled with disco lights.

When the band finishes, we make our way through the steep, winding streets, climb in the car, and head home. I stretch out as much as the caricature of a back seat will allow, Yugos not being built for comfort or speed, and watch the mountain silhouettes slip by. Their voices are a comforting buzz in the front seat, the radio a quiet hum holding us all up. I feel easy in my skin, in their company. *Breathe in, breathe out, stay in the moment. Breathe in, breathe out, stay in the moment.* It's a mantra that is playing in my head, and though I don't remember saying it to myself, it's good advice. *Breathe in, breathe out, watch their profiles, feel the laughter, this is real, stay in the moment.* I remember the smell of ghee candles, playing in the melted wax and wondering at the differences of temperature while my parents and their friends chanted and meditated. Heat without being burned. *Breathe in, breathe out, stay in the moment.*

# Sanctuary

I wake up when the wheels crunch over the gravel of their driveway, lever myself out of the back seat and follow them inside. All the cozy warmth of the club and the car have dissipated, and the trailer is as cold as the outside. The heater went out while we were gone, and Linda goes down the hall to try to get the pilot light going. The cold plus the realization of bedtime combine to bring me wide awake. All the easy confidence drains out, leaving anxious chilly shivers in its wake. Denise notices and bundles me up in a blanket, one arm around my shoulders while she and Linda consult along the length of the hallway. The final consensus is that the heat isn't coming back on quickly enough and that it's far too cold for me to sleep alone on the couch. The three of us will share their bed and stay warm. I'm following them down the hall and wondering if I'm still drowsing in the car or perhaps completely misunderstanding them and about to make a fool of myself. Maybe this is a test, to see if I'm honorable. Or a test to see if I'm too much of a novice to accept. Or a test...of whether I like Sade? There's a life-size poster, beautifully lit, taped to the ceiling over their bed. I'm short enough to see most of it standing up, but it's obvious it's best viewed lying down.

I'm clutching my blanket around me in the doorway, trying not to stare at everything, trying not to stare at them. Linda piles two more quilts on the bed and then another pillow while Denise unwinds me. "Don't worry," she says, "there's plenty of room." They strip down to T-shirts and underwear, as do I, though mine are the only ones that involve lace. I don't know where to be or how to act, though I do feel safe, even in my confusion. They put me between them, three spoons in a row, pull up the covers, and turn out the lights. I feel like all those sleepovers in high school, my friend asleep and me afraid to close my eyes, afraid I'll reach out in my dreams, betray my thoughts, cross the line. I can feel Denise fall off to sleep, her breath going deep and slow, her muscles relaxing back against me. Linda is a live wire behind me, held in check, her hands shifting, then freezing, not touching, not touching. I can feel her desire like a heater against my back. The long muscles in her thighs tense and release and I'm sure I'll never sleep, hung on the edge of possibility like this. And then sunlight and Denise smiling down at me.

She reaches out her hand and lays it against my breastbone, fingers splayed and pressing down just a little. She raises one eyebrow and my mouth goes dry, and her smile quirks into a grin. She opens a drawer and starts pulling out bundles, wrapped in handkerchiefs, and placing them on the bed. She starts unwrapping them as she tells Linda that we should go take a shower and freshen up, and as I'm processing that, the first bandanna falls open and I see purple sparkling strangeness in a familiar shape, see her wrap her hand around it for a moment, and then we're out the door. My brain is spinning as Linda starts the water, finds some towels, and tests the temperature. She reaches out to pull my T-shirt over my head, and my eyes go wide. The steam on the bathroom mirror, the running water, the charge in the air. She doesn't know my history, but she is paying attention. Linda takes my hand, looks me in the eye, breathes with me. "You can say no at any time." I look away and back, and her face is a brightness I can hardly look at, but I do. "This is a gift we want to give you."

I take off my T-shirt, my panties, and step into the shower, holding the curtain open for her. She strips quickly and steps in with me.

She puts her hand on my shoulder and feels me tense, waits for me to relax again, and pulls me into a hug. She holds me in the water, not grasping, not invading. Just skin. Just water.

I pull back, and she lets me go immediately, standing naked and eyes open before me. Waiting. I tilt up my face and she gives me a kiss, soft and endless and wet and then tongues and nibbling and the water and her hot mouth until the water runs cold. We towel ourselves to warm again and hurry back down the hallway. Denise not only got the heat to turn on but has lit candles and put on music. The wide bed has fresh sheets, and there are several more interesting unwrapped bundles in the pile on the nightstand. She is naked under a short satin robe, her skin gleaming. I feel impossibly high and reckless and beautiful, and then Denise lowers her mouth to mine, and I swoon. Linda is standing right behind me, and between them they lay me down on the bed. I've never been so well kissed, and it's endless. One mouth on mine, one nibbling my neck, my shoulder, down to my breasts, and I'm shuddering. Wet hair, wet tongues, my toes sucked, my lips bitten, four hands, and I'm breathless and in sensory overload, and they feel it. Stop. Hold me. Breathe. Start again.

It feels like hours, like days, like the longest moment of indrawn breath. I haven't had an orgasm since Samantha, my nerves clamping down about halfway to any peak, nothing but white noise and flatline. Not even my own hands can find the way. One by one, their fingers, twining with each other inside me. One by one, the toys, wielded gently, firmly, deeply. Denise has moved downward, licking and biting my thighs while her hand glides in, out, around, wait, wait, plunge, twist, her hair a soft cloud against my hip. Linda bears the brunt of my long straight-girl nails, scratches and welts along her back and forearms, her mouth is around my nipple, and there are stars behind my eyelids.

## SOSSITY CHIRICUZIO

A rush is building at my core like an earthquake, like a flash flood, and it feels like I'm breaking down a wall with the crown of my head. So much pleasure cresting, such a reservoir of pain. I'm panting and animal moans and flushed to the waist. A train without brakes around the curve, never mind the piles of dynamite or the victim tied across the tracks. Never mind the nerve endings I haven't forgiven. Never mind, there's no mind, there's nothing but sparks flying across darkness and a breath I can't pull past my closed throat until I can, and then I scream and come and again and still more, ripples slapping back into one another, let loose like a landslide until I'm crying and begging for silence. For stillness. I can't see, my vision full of lightning and salt water. They curl around me, sanctuary.

# Single wide trailer

Sun drenching down from the picture window on stretched out naked limbs, lungs heavy and happy with the rumbling, tumbling smoke of a four-foot graphic bong, hair clean and air-drying. Graveyard shift exhausted. Smiling.

This trailer, wider, quieter, higher on a hill, is well worth the extra $30 a month my mother pitches in to give me a place of peace. A place to rest between dispatching cabs, running to class, exploring love.

One driver lays his obsession on me, another cleans a pound of pot on my kitchen table, another plots to make me late enough to lose my job. Takes my job. Frees me from my job. I scrimp and wait and smile.

Two months until university, the big city, thousands of people I've never met, who know none of my stories, have witnessed none of my shame. Two months of chrysalis until my unfolding. I lie in the sun and dream of wings.

# Up a tree

The dorm is shaped like a giant X. Boy, girl, boy, girl, floor after floor. I live on the very top left, all the way at the end. All of my possessions and questions and expressions in one hundred fifty square feet of space. Half a room of brick walls and furniture older than me. I cover it with plants and posters. My art leaks across to the other side of the room, mingles with ease. My mother and I are much alike and make really good roommates. Surprising everyone, especially since the latest news in the halls is that I'm gay.

They assumed maybe we were sisters, then lovers, and now it's confirmed she's my mother. Still a weirdo, no longer caring. We want to learn about the same things, we enjoy the same music, have lots of community overlap. We take turns going for long walks or trips to the library when lovers come to visit, and we both smoke weed but not in the room. Her less often, mostly at parties, but it's a medicine both physical and mental for me. Not the easiest thing to disguise in a dorm, and I don't like to be rushed about it.

I finally find a solution, across the bike lane, in a grove of olive trees shading the west side of the campus. They are sturdy, easy to climb, and empty of anyone else but me and the birds. I find a good perch at least ten feet up, usually just after dusk, settle in with my pipe and watch the sky. The smoke doesn't travel down, and nobody looks up. Carving out spaces like this for myself makes it possible to live in the middle of such a crowd. After my trailer for one, five hundred housemates is a little hard to take, even when one of them is my best friend.

It wasn't an instant shift from surly teenager to fellow adult, but we've sorted through the hardest stuff and made some good boundaries. We're both in the middle of huge transformations, and it's comforting to share them. She's finding her way back to art and herself as a person outside of mothering, of spousing. I'm finding my way back into my skin, learning how to stay present and absorb knowledge all at once. There's so much to find out about the world, about myself, and about how to change them both.

We both take every humanities class available and fall in (philosophical) love with the same professor. She is smart, persistent, and gracious, a potent combination even if she weren't giving us permission to talk passionately about art, human nature, and culture. We reverberate off each other in class, pass dog-eared books back and forth, grow intoxicated with knowledge and dialog. We take core classes around the edges, the ones that will turn this treasure hunt into a degree, but what we both want are answers and fellow questioners. A chance to redefine ourselves.

Rose begins to find fellow artists and activists, to go to potlucks, to build a new community of creative souls and outlets. I join the Gay and Lesbian Alliance, try to untangle myself from my affair with Linda, to find my way to an intimacy that doesn't come with lying to Denise or myself. I know it's my own doing, but I can't even remember why it ever seemed like a choice I could live with or why it felt worth it. To be wanted enough to take that kind of risk is some sort of poisonous proof that I'm desirable, but the secret letters and clandestine meetings have become a mass of sharp edges and sorrow.

I busy myself with class, with feminism, with learning my way around college and all the secret places to smoke weed or have a moment's privacy, with one student aid job after another. Serving food to alumni and spoiled jocks, bow tie and resentment tight around my throat. Shelving books in the science library, endless aisles of facts and sexual frustration. Pictograms and phone numbers scratched into every desk surface a testament to the thwarted hours passing slowly. Everywhere hormones and posturing and ego and need, and I, swimming through it, trying to find a place where skin is safe again.

Summer rushes up on us, and we realize we will shortly have to vacate our room in entirety, that our break will mean the end of a space in time of sharing. We begin to pack and store and transport all our pieces of home to safe places, prepare our plan B. I apply for a queer summer activist training camp in San Francisco, never expecting to get in, so when I do, the scramble for funds and a ride is fast but successful. I drop some things at my mother's house and some with a friend of Denise and Linda's where I settle in as a temporary nanny until my adventure in the homeland of gay where I will surely figure myself out.

# Queer activist training camp

The truck is faded red, but his smile is brilliant. Will is also headed to the activist gathering and has scooped me up along the way. The day passes in laughter and conversation and miles rolling easy under the wheels on this road to discovery. Belted in between us is the little girl I've been nannying, on her way to her grandparents' for the summer, listening to us sometimes but mostly watching the desert change colors outside the window.

We pull into a road stop for lunch, smoke a joint on the tailgate while she stretches tiny legs in big looping circles like the topography lines of the map we check our exits on. We drive on for hours, dusk floating down over the old mountains so slowly we share another three years' worth of personal story before the stars show through. Leaving her shining in the middle of a crowd of cousins, we turn the hood toward San Francisco and transformation.

Will is clearly comfortable in his body in a way I barely remember. He knows his beauty but doesn't bother to look for it in the mirror; talks of lovers as if they are plentiful; gently corrects my language when I stumble. He makes this enormous adventure feel safe and doesn't disappear even when we get to the city full of beautiful boys. I take dozens of photos of him, tagging along on walks full of sunlight and surprise kisses.

They put us all up in college dorms, and we are paired off in rooms with much laughter about the ridiculous overlap of our queer truths and the university's rules about gender. I am sharing a room with an androgynous lesbian who seems as confused by me as I am, or maybe that's just me tripping over myself again. Even in this crowd of colorful, cheerful deviants, I still feel other. Still feel myself hovering at the edges, watching for clues on how to be.

I gravitate toward other fringe dwellers in the room, finding out they are often also perverts and bookworms and outlaws and geeks. We swap skills for organizing protests and safe sex, praise one another's costumes and vocabulary of curses, tumble into a curious pile of nerve endings and BDSM one afternoon to learn about power and hedonism and taking turns. We are unsure, we are jubilant, we are tearful, we are loud.

In the afternoons, we meet in caucus, and I'm the last to pick myself for a team every time. I live in the overlaps, and they are knots of certainty. I try to participate but mostly listen, and when we're done, I seek a quiet place to absorb it all. Sitting alone on balconies, in spots of shade behind large boulders, in small empty rooms – I don't want to miss a moment of it, but I'm oversaturated. Too many choices after making myself fit in a small world.

The experience is an enormous and dense patchwork of political actions and contemplative conversations, rubbing our various levels of radical against one another while we seek common language and potential for collaboration. While we learn there is no utopia. While we rage against racist bar owners and homophobic newspapers and every level of government as the wave of death floods our community.

We weep together as the quilt is laid out in a million squares of heartbreak and lives cut short.

We scream together at the sky.

## SOSSITY CHIRICUZIO

We strip down naked and swim together in the private pool of a rich lesbian who lives among the redwoods – more breasts and cunts and cocks than many of us have ever seen, regardless of which we long for. We splash and sing and laugh as if we're in no danger at all, almost believing it for one long, sun-drenched afternoon. We later stake out a spot on the public beach for watching fireworks and shout down a few bigots who can't seem to count.

In the evenings, our elders come – performers and poets and philosophers, faeries and flannel and firebrands – bringing stories we thought we were only just now writing and reminders of how to maybe survive them. We listen to Pansy Division, read yellowed and brittle copies of the *Mattachine Review* and *The Ladder*, and debate topics like separatism, homogenization, and language.

We take our classes in a UU church just off Castro and have two hours a day to wander the neighborhood. It's all rainbow all the time, glorious and freeing and increasingly highlighting the tiny, dim and painstakingly carved out cave I usually exist in. In Tucson, you're gay or lesbian, country or rock, androgynous or slightly less so. There, my femme gender is invisible, especially when I pick up a power tool, and my desire for multiple partners makes me suspect in every group.

The summer is winding down, and I never want to be less than I am right this moment, but I can already feel myself holding back and shrinking back down. *On Our Backs* invites a group of the dyke-identified folks to do an erotic photo shoot, and I can't think of anything I'd rather do…and I can imagine the explosion of it colliding with Linda's paranoia and suspicion. I opt out, knowing that the compromises won't stop there but lost as to how to reconcile it all.

# Where secrets always lodge

She's angry and reckless and so very high, eighteen lines in eight hours, all of Southern California a blur of headlights on the highway and paranoia given rein. I'm exhausted, terrified, trapped. Linda showed up by surprise, dumped her suitcase on my dorm bed and ordered a pizza. She said she came to drive me home. I had another week of summer camp, no room for her, not ready to get back in the tiny, tidy little box that made her feel safe. Not ready maybe ever again.

She said it would be romantic. Gave my roommate a long, sharp look that sent them out the door, mumbling a reason. Pummeled me with lovemaking I hadn't missed after all. Unpacked her suitcase, ate the pizza, didn't leave my side.

My roommate found a new room. I asked people to be nice to Linda, not to tell her about our shared adventures. Feeling the ice growing in the roof of my mouth, where secrets always lodge. Not sure what I was hiding or asking for. Knowing she would explode at any opportunity. Their eyes changed, looking at me. Pity and distance. Such a fall from fierce young activist. From sexy comrade. She wanted all my sexy safe in hand. Installed an on/off switch. Threatened to disconnect my power.

Five minutes of silence in the truck, five days later, and I start to drift off. She taps the brakes, hard, so I jerk in my seat belt. Asks me if I want us to die. If I'm trying to make her crazy. My heart is beating almost as fast as hers and my foot is pressing, pressing the floorboard.

## SOSSITY CHIRICUZIO

She says she is only doing this for me. That the meth is so she can drive me home. That if I hadn't gone so far away she wouldn't need it. That if I don't help her stay awake we'll crash and die. That if I wouldn't flirt with people she wouldn't need to break into my trunk, read my diary, question my friends, track me down. That if I would just be grateful for all she does, maybe we could be happy. That nobody will ever love me like she does. That nobody ever loved her right.

Her words squeak out between clenched teeth and her knuckles are white on the wheel. Inside the cab, outside the window, only streaks of light, showing nothing. Seven more hours until I am home. Three more weeks until summer's end, and ours. I pinch my fingers to bleeding and count.

# Fault lines

I'm still not sure exactly how that sanctuary turned into a shadowy place. No, that's not true. It started when Denise and Linda teased me about being on the fence when I didn't claim the word lesbian right away. I wanted to, just as I wanted everything about who they are, but I already feel so young and unsure and out of my element. I have nothing to contribute except my company and help around the house. They are introducing me to feminist theory and lesbian music and politics and sex, and I want it all, but sometimes it's also too much after years of being so locked down.

One day, they tell me they love me. That we all fit so good together and they want to welcome me into their life. To marry them and move in and grow into whatever this is between us. I have never felt so wanted or so trapped all at once. I mumble something about thinking about it and make an exit so fast I'm blocks away before I realize what I've done. I avoid them for a week, trying to wrap my head around it, but by the time I finally come back, the damage is done. They are very gentle about it, no shaming involved, but they say it's clear it was too much and that I'm not ready and that we should all try to figure out how to just be friends.

I'm so angry at myself and on the outside looking in again. Back to sleeping on the couch and watching them kiss. Back to useless attempts to make myself come and a rising tide of numb. Back to being hungry for intimacy all the time.

One day, when Denise is out shopping, Linda surprises me with a kiss. I'm so lost in the feel of it that I don't even think to question it, but when she pulls away, she tells me not to say anything about it. That she loves me and misses me and can't stand to not touch me but that Denise doesn't want us to be lovers anymore. That she'll go crazy if she can't be with me, but she'd die without Denise. That if I really love her, I'll do anything it takes to make it work.

My body is alive with desire, but my brain is frozen in place. It's all I can do to nod before we hear the tires of the Yugo pulling into the driveway, and Linda is pushing me toward the couch and rushing back to the sink, kissing Denise when she brings in the groceries, acting as if nothing at all has changed while I sink into the couch and a pit of shame. I swear to myself I will resist, that I'll just explain to Linda I can't lie like that, but the next time she gets a moment alone with me I find myself coming on her strong fingers while the blood pounds behind my eyes, and I swallow the sounds we used to all delight in.

These stolen moments splatter all over the summer months and my ragged conscience, and I find myself ever more eager to escape to school, knowing the hour and a half to Tucson will make it close to impossible to find time, sure that this will just stop if I can get far enough away to resist temptation and comfort and desire. I am sick with the secret, with sex being about secrets, with a desire I have to hide. All the shine they laid on my skin is tarnishing, and my capacity to lie makes mirrors impossible and eating a waste. I can hardly look at Denise, which is a loss all its own, and I begin to wonder if there's any good in me after all.

Finally summer ends, and the rush to school begins, and I leave it all behind me with more than a little relief. I settle in, start to look for friends and myself again, stuffing any thoughts of Linda or Denise into a tiny space at the back of my mind. Until the letter arrives. Pages and pages of love and frustration and desire and jealousy and sorrow in Linda's looping handwriting, mailed from a postbox and filled with detailed instructions on how to reply. She's beguiled their neighbor to be our postmaster, and the number of ways I'm supposed to pine and prove myself are many and tangled.

I feel dizzy, like I can't catch my breath, like I should be running away, but I already did, and it seems there is no escape. She painstakingly plans a trip to Tucson to bring me the last of my stuff, sending letter after letter full of details on how we'll lock ourselves in my dorm room and make love for hours. It doesn't really feel like love anymore, though, or if it's love, it's the kind that breaks you. I try to explain my sense of shame, my need to be honest, my hope for growth, but it all translates to her as betrayal and rejection and she begins to talk of hurting herself. Of how I'm hurting her, sending me Polaroids of herself covered in quotes of things I said to her and words like "forever" and "mine."

My entire semester becomes a schism of knowledge and secrecy, growing toward what I want and clipping myself down to what she wants. I begin to hate her, already hating myself. I even begin to be angry at Denise for not seeing it or stopping it. I know there is nothing fair about any of these feelings, and I have nobody to talk to about it. My mother looks at me with worry in her eyes but doesn't tell me what to do – part of the way we've learned to live together as friends, rather than parent and child. I wish she would, though. I know she would agree that this is not right and that we all deserve better, and I want to ask her, and I want to figure it out on my own, and I want to disappear.

The semester is winding down, and we can't stay in the dorms during summer break. Everything I own is going back to that tiny city, as am I, until the summer adventure of queer politics begins. Six weeks of uninhibited sexuality and knowledge and activism await me; I just have to persevere until I can break free of her orbit once again. I surround myself with company, refuse dinner invitations at their trailer, try hard to gently disengage without bringing the entire house of cards down around us. I flee to San Francisco and hope it will somehow dissolve while I'm gone.

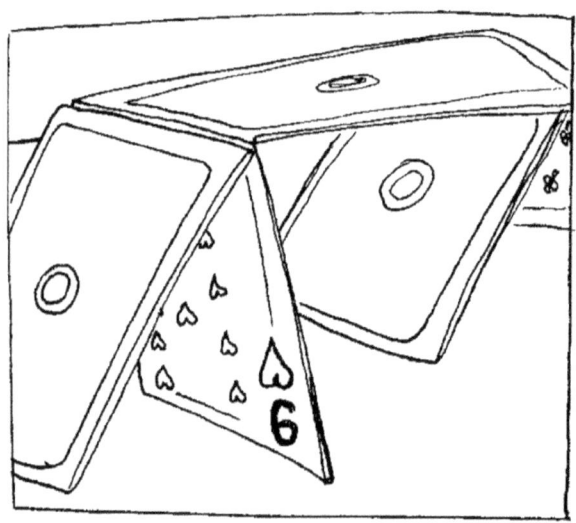

When I finally get back to school, I opt to find an apartment instead of the dorms and settle into a tiny duplex in biking distance of the college. The letters keep coming. I pull back further and further, trying to ease out of this tangled mess and into my own life, but the lie has gotten too big, and the secret finally slips out. Denise finds a letter, gets the truth out of Linda, packs up her half of their things, drives her up to Tucson, and drops her on my doorstep saying, "You wanted her, now you have her."

Denise's look of disappointment is every bit as sharp as I'd been imagining for a year now, and Linda is a mess. She's lost everything, and somehow it's all my fault. She moves in and fills my home with despair and rage and resentment and expectation. Everything I do is less right than how Denise would do it. Everything I have to offer is shabby in comparison, and she doesn't really want to be here but explodes at the thought of leaving, demanding to know how can I think of turning her away when she did all of this for me?

The sex becomes angry, becomes control, becomes something she gives, or takes away, depending on a myriad of things. Suspecting my loyalty, my love, even my acts of kindness. She wrenches her back, ends up in a temporary wheelchair, accuses me of enjoying the power of pushing her around. She comes to me crying from a knot in her stomach that never lets go, and I curl around her, kneading at the mass of memory and misery she carries there. Shutting down every nerve ending but the ones in my fingers, making myself a wall inside soft skin.

She gets a job, an apartment, gives me a set of keys, holds out her hand for a set of mine. She wants to know everything I do, meet everyone I know, disparages most of it when we're alone. She praises my perversion and then withholds it. She calls me her fuck monster. She calls me her consolation prize. Tells me I sound like Traci Lords when I come. Tells me to stop coming.

We break apart, slide back together, jagged edges seeking comfort, split harder every time. One night she hurls her vacuum past me, tumbling down the hallway like a plastic landslide, and then stands between me and her door, raging at some other inherent fault of my entire being, refusing to let me leave, and I feel something shift irrevocably inside me. She paces and rants for another twenty minutes while I sit quiet on the edge of a bed that used to hold love and wait for her to wind down. My lack of response finally registers. I see her see me, done with this. I pick up my backpack, walk toward her, hold out my hand. She lays my keys across my palm; I lay hers on the windowsill and close the door behind me.

# Brown-eyed girl

She is so many things I wish I could've been. She is out and proud and supported in her alternative school. She is confident that she is worthy of love, and she lives in a city big enough to find some. She is seventeen, and she is always watching me.

Not too much younger to smoke weed with, but definitely too much younger to kiss, even though she asks me so sweetly. She's mature for her age, she keeps reminding me, and if she were nineteen and I were twenty-one, it wouldn't matter. But we aren't, and it does.

The sunroof on her car is open to let the smoke out, and Edie Brickell croons on the tape deck about how philosophy is a walk on slippery rocks, and her flickering grin makes that feel all too true. I want her to have a first that is kind and present and her own age. She wants me.

She makes me a copper pendant that matches one of my tattoos, inscribing her love on the back in a shaky but determined hand. She makes me a cassette tape full of her thoughts to take to queer boot camp. She makes me laugh. She makes me wonder.

I make her wait. I am trying so hard to do the right thing, to be the older, wiser, helpful friend. To accept her desire as a compliment and her friendship as a gift and safeguard the innocence she wants to spend on me. She turns eighteen soon, she reminds me, every time we meet.

I am still too tangled in Linda, my edges jagged and dangerous. I am still sorting out the sweet from the dangerous in my own barely eighteen adventure and all the aftershocks of it. I am still afraid to do her damage, still afraid of my own damage.

She tires of waiting and dives into a bad choice of a first. Linda figured she could take out the competition and notch another conquest in one fell swoop. She survives it much better than I. She lets it go. She shows me what that looks like. She tells me she still wants me. She waits.

The pool is perfectly blue, totally private. Her brown eyes are radiant in the sunshine, her teeth flash in a grin that holds nothing of shyness. She strips out of her jumpsuit, walks into the water, slides her arms underneath me and offers me up to the wide sky. Naked and unafraid.

# Radical sex

I wasn't the only young Scorpio femme who had been figuring it out at queer boot camp, and Cecily and I were drawn to each other like magnets. We were both searching among bohemian and punk to find our look, tough enough to be tomboys but in love with dangly earrings and glittery scarves and lace bras. In love with whatever femme was while we figured it out and made it up.

A year later, she was finishing up a degree at Grinell, looking for her next adventure, and swooped through Tucson to take me to Mardi Gras in New Orleans. I hadn't driven those southern roads since the post high school road trip, and to do so with another radical queer was surreal and such a gift. She splurged on me, showed me the town, flirted gently.

Lovers or friends? Friends and lovers? Romance or perversion or subversion or all of the above? It took us trial and error and trust to figure it out, but we're now pretty solid as housemates, friends, and occasional playmates. We wrestle, we laugh, we cook dinner, we tag-team on adventurous butches. We trip out on various drugs and endorphins and honesty.

Her good friend Veronica, also in Tucson by way of Grinell, is our third housemate, and collectively we rabble-rouse and deviate our way through the local scene. We attend a potluck on women's land but get asked to leave for wearing leather boots. We help throw a play party in the local NOW office. We host skill-swap gatherings of leather dykes and curious lesbians.

Sometimes we dress outrageously and go to the shopping mall on a Sunday and make out in public places. Sometimes we are covert (the night they spray paint "Queer looking, queer acting, seeks same" along 4th Avenue), and sometimes we are overt (the day I free bleed all along University Drive), and sometimes we just howl at the moon.

We share lovers and sex tips and comfort food recipes, best days and worst days and deepest secrets. We weather conflict and jealousy and pull apart and come back together. We adorn the house and one another. We meet one another's parents and inner children. We make mistakes, we learn to name them, we learn to let them go.

Cecily moves in with a lover, Veronica, and I move into a duplex. We grow apart, we grow back together. We keep reaching toward truth and hedonism and revolution. We watch one another weather heartbreak and crisis and self-doubt and dangerous choices, respecting autonomy with aching hearts. We patch one another up after, stitches set by loving hands.

# The high cost of education

I brought all the anger and awareness of my time in San Francisco back with me, and it is stretching the seams of my life. I find myself fighting as much as studying, and there's just no such thing as a simple conversation anymore. Everything is connected, and most of it feels broken. I argue with first-wave feminists about porn and penetration, with people in the Gay and Lesbian Alliance about adding bisexual to the name, with professors about the specialized and exclusive language we're supposed to write and dialog with. I find myself unable to share what I'm learning without making most of my friends and family feel ignorant, which is the opposite of what I want out of education.

What I want is to know about all the things that school never saw fit to teach me before. What I want is to challenge the systems that prioritize order over discussion and grades over knowledge. What I want is to make a difference, and I'm no longer sure I can do that within this system. My thoughts of becoming a professor are starting to feel like hobbles, and all I can think about is kicking down the gates.

I had gotten involved with the local chapter of Queer Nation, and when I heard about their latest action, I knew I had to be a part of it. Arizona law states that a woman's nipples are obscene, and if someone under the age of fifteen sees and complains, it could land you on the sex offenders list. The hypocrisy of this, and the commodification and control of women's bodies, is what is obscene, and I am far from the only one to think so. A Tit-In is planned, and I join dozens of women and men on the campus mall in the bright sunshine, and we all remove our shirts. Because of the law, all of the women have their nipples covered, and most of the men do too in solidarity.

The majority of the women are slender, with large pieces of tape covering most of their small breasts, but I chose the smallest Band-Aids in the box, decorated with Oscar from *Sesame Street*, and made an X across my nipples. My breasts are a double D, but my nipples are small, and I'm determined to obey only the barest letter of the law. It's effective, but once again I find myself too much for most of the other outlaws.

The air on my skin, something I'd usually enjoy, is a reminder of how vulnerable I am. These are fellow students and teachers, and I'm not really sure who is seeing me because there are so many of them. It's all I can do not to cross my arms over my chest like so many others are doing, and I'm trying hard to be brave. Just as I start to feel like I might not be able to do this, I notice that none of the men staring at me are making eye contact. For men to overlook my eyes in favor of staring at my tits is not a new thing, but right now it's exaggerated to such a degree that I realize it's not just about them dismissing my personhood but also being afraid of it.

I fix my gaze on a small group and walk toward them, slowly but deliberately. They notice, start to shift, looking up and away, quick glances that refuse to land on my face. The closer I get, the more panicky they look, until they suddenly disperse in different directions away from me. Not looking back, not exchanging comments about my body, not making me feel small or unsafe. I feel transformed. My feet become roots, dug deep, my face the sun.

The idea of my vulnerability being a strength is not new, but I've never considered it in the sense of political action before. That these men, whom I would likely fear if it were dark or I were alone, practically ran away from me is so powerful I feel intoxicated. I look around and see that other women are discovering this as well. I hear voices getting louder and see that a group of frat boys have zeroed in on one of our protesters, but before we can help, she lifts her breasts in her hands and steps into their personal space, calling them bullies and cowards in a calm but carrying tone. They step back, she steps forward again, and again, faster each time until they are actually running away. Her smile is glorious, we are all glorious in the bright light.

The Tit-In lasts all semester and costs me several classes' worth of credit but teaches me more about myself and direct action and collaborative protests than anything in the college catalog. I get involved in the Women's Resource Center, in Take Back The Night, in every panel or protest or project that is about changing the status quo and challenging the layers upon layers of codified bias in our curriculums and structure.

My professors generally like me, even though they find me challenging, and while my papers are full of red ink for lowercase "i" and colloquialisms and opinion-based writing, they are also full of encouragement for my passion and perseverance and point of view. We have a respectful but wary relationship – they know I will call things out and am not awed by authority but also that I do it in search of knowledge, not nuisance. It's becoming increasingly clear that the ladder they are climbing to reach a place of being heard is not for me, and given my ongoing conflicts with the college administration and student council, it's unlikely I could make myself follow the rules that are required for any sort of job security.

The website I've built for the Women's Resource Center is the latest source of contention. I've hot-linked some of the text to radical resources and am being called in for a meeting about the content involved. "Self-defense" takes you to Hothead Paisan, and "body image" takes you to FatSo! There are many other links, but apparently, they are so freaked out by homicidal lesbian cartoons and naked butts that they can't get past them to even critique the rest.

We're all sitting in this beige room and I can't believe this is important enough for this kind of trouble and time, and they can't believe I'm not apologizing or ashamed. These are the people who make diversity groups compete for funding, who police their events and language but never lift them up or include them without a fight. These people are shocked that they inspire neither respect nor fear in me and that I am willing to defend my choices for hours on end if need be. That I found the loophole in their last set of restrictions and passed out their email addresses to anyone else who found the links and free will reasonable. That technically I didn't do anything wrong and can't be punished for it.

I'm living on knowledge and anger and one large cup of frozen yogurt a day – all the lunch my budget will allow for – and I savor all of them, licking my lips for the ghost of the flavors as the weeks wear on. I'm poking holes in the very system I hoped would save me from manual labor and finding that my truth lines up more with what I can do with my hands. That my worth will have to be found out in the world.

# Heartsister

Mary appears in my life like a sunrise. Magnificent and startling and utterly familiar. She sees me. Bone deep and laid bare. Beautiful. She calls me beautiful, lets me see it in her eyes. She shows me femme in motion, badass and graceful and ragged and timeless.

Deep-black eyeliner and a chain from ear to nose, her profile could slice you to ribbons, no less so her tongue. She is so smart it hurts, and she uses it as both a pen and a blade. Peeling away layers of lies, cracking tradition at the seams and testing for poison.

She is so strong that just about every butch and boy wants to lie down at her feet, which sounds like a compliment until you see how much lifting is involved. Like me, she loves taking someone apart and building them back up again. Like me, she gets tired.

She mirrors the goddess in me. The fiercely feminine divine. The almost bottomless well. The glory and weight of our succulence, how people want to feast but mostly in secret. She sees the feral kitten in me. The cracks in the bucket and the blisters on my hands.

She lets me hold her. Curling her length against me and crying. Her tears taste like mine. The salt of loving our bodies even when others can't figure out how. Of stepping outside the system of competition and scarcity even though it means we sometimes starve.

My name in her mouth feels like benediction. Like a hundred reasons to keep living. Like I am so much more than all the ways I've been torn down. Like I am not too much. My name in her mouth is always love, even in the moments when I stumble.

# Gentlebutch

No taller than me, soft spoken, soft lines in a friendly face, she's leading an entire country bar in a sequence of steps that looks intriguing and challenging all at once. My body wants to dance but is frozen stiff, remembering those numb circles across the floor locked in Linda's arms. How it felt like my knees forgot how to bend or my neck to unbend. How I could hear the grace but not feel it.

I realize I've drifted closer to the dance floor when she catches my eye and smiles, beckoning me over. I smile but shake my head, but she's already walking toward me – "Come dance!" – while she tucks my hand under her elbow, and I'm walking toward the center of the crowd, and she slides me into the line behind her so I can watch what she's doing. The blood is pounding in my ears but I can still hear the beat and I'm stepping sideways, and back, and not bumping into anyone else and we all spin to the left and I can feel the music and she's smiling and I'm smiling and when the music switches to a waltz there I am, in her arms. Easy.

She counts for me at first, but I'm already relaxing into her lead, letting her move me backward without craning my neck. Trusting her. My long skirt is twirling outward, showing off my fishnets and steel-tipped boots, and my cleavage is taking on a sheen of sweat, and her eyes are firmly fixed on my own. No struggle involved, she is courtly to the core.

I start coming once a week, twice a week, early for lessons before the crowd comes in, becoming her first-choice partner for teaching couple dances and spending most of the evening in her arms.

She can two-step or three-step or waltz to anything, twirling me to Prince and Madonna and even Chaka Khan those few times the DJ gives in to prodding and drops a rock block in the mix. One hand holding mine, the other on the small of my back, guiding but never caressing, never slipping downward, never pulling me close. I cherish feeling graceful, feeling beautiful and sought out for nothing more than a willingness to trust and spin, making infinite spirals on the wooden floor.

I also flirt, just a little, now and again. She enjoys the attention but deflects anything direct. She's thirty years my senior and very aware of it; a lifelong teacher just now getting to be out and proud. She invites me over for dinner, shares stories of her teenage trysts with the daughters of pastors and mayors, her love of teaching, and the pressure of being closeted for so long.

In her living room hangs a portrait from her early twenties, blond ducktail sleek over bright blue eyes and a strong jawline, dreamy like James Dean. She smiles at me from across the kitchen and I know I've been welcomed into her intimate space as far as I will go. She changes the subject whenever my compliments take on any hint of heat, and I respect that boundary, though I wish I could trail kisses along the seams of her wrinkles and that still-proud jawline, full of gratitude for the ground she broke and the ground she made smooth. For her gentle arms and her unwavering courtesy. For twirling me back into grace.

# Meeting at the crossroads

Motorcycle hum thrumming between my legs, ripped jeans channeling wind along my calves and the desert blurring past us like a golden dream. My arms around Sam. Her thick back a safe place to rest my head. Her heart a safe place too.

We are friends. We are flirting with more than that but reluctant to dive into deep waters while she is packing to move away. We are art and acid trips and watermelon, wet defiance in the sunshine. We are leather jackets among the flannel. We are not falling in love.

She meets my family and is family. She takes me seriously and makes me giggle. Makes me mixed tapes of longing and letting go. I shave designs into her palm-tickling buzz cut, showering us both with glittering hairs that linger for days.

# Last night in town

She comes on strong; it's her baseline. Having convinced me to come over for a joint, she tries to make a case for staying the night. Offering but not handing over cab fare, flirting with a heavy hand, but ultimately giving it up as Scorpio stubbornness meets itself coming and going.

I'm totally her type, I am given to understand. Caretaking mama femme who can be flipped over, but not always. She was a long-time love of Mary's, which makes me wary, intrigued, and extra hands off. The kind of flame that could easily burn everyone in reach. For over a year, I think better of it. Watch how she gets possessive even never having possessed, watch how she watches me. But those big hands, those knowing looks. Being wanted so intensely is still new, and her air of danger feels like a test I want to pass.

She's the bouncer at the cool nightclub downtown, her curly crew cut, tattoos, piercings, and beard making her almost more than the locals can handle, which helps keep them in line. She's capital B Butch, with a collection of curses gleaned from London to Germany and back.

Tucson ultimately feels too small-town, and she decides to move to Provincetown. Her last night is a work shift, and she invites me to come keep her company. Twenty-seven hundred miles feels like an insurance policy against drama and an opportunity to explore, with Mary's blessing in hand. I show up at midnight wearing red lace everything, short shorts, and a grin with no holds barred.

She's surprised, her coworkers are impressed, and I am awash in the feeling of my own daring. Totally not out of control, just wild because I want to be.

I dance for her until we're both sweating then press my body against hers and my key into her hand. Invite her to let herself in and wake me up when her shift is over. Savor the surprise and hunger chasing across her face and walk away slow and swinging.

I wake to her teeth working crescents across the skin of my back, already shuddering and slick with it. She is solid pounding waves behind me, fingers sunk deep in my hip and a stream of profane endearments pouring into my ear like poetry, making me cry with need. Later, I am astride her, moving so slow she'd beg me to stop, or speed up, if she weren't such a masochist. Taking it, waiting for it, giving it up. Striving to be good while reveling in being bad. Finding power in giving it away. These are magic spells we both understand.

For this one night we revel in it. Grabbing and giving with both hands. Marks stitch across our skin like the map she'll follow in the morning, dips and curves and wide-open spaces. Everything sweet and sore and sticky. Everything sacred.

# Stars and steam

The room is wood and breathes in the night air. The air is heat waves and liquid and wordless songs. Naked skin, scent of mesquite, water hissing on pumice. Sweating like a prayer.

A secret grove in the middle of the city, rich with trees and silence. Deep cool pool of water reflecting the stars. Hammocks spiraling around it all, slow rocking.

The sweating is memories. Is salt tears rising. Is deep release. The sweating is sacred. Is blasphemy. Is constellations of vulnerability.

Water as reckoning. As refuge. As rebirth. Submerged and saturated. Swallowing and swallowed. Rivulets and rivers and roaring waves and ripples and raindrops.

We come together like strangers. Make magic like sisters. Whisper stories and solidarity through the trees. Trade herbs and tinctures and crystals and names. Scrawl poetry by starlight.

# Thunderstorm

Storm comes through Tucson midsummer, full of lightning-tongued charm. Accent thick like the porcelain cocks she makes, swirled with color and smooth enough to lull you into forgetting what thunder feels like. She straps one to her forehead, kneels before the sling strung in our living room, finds her way inside me by the heat of her third eye.

This summer is queer magic piled on top of ritual piled on top of hormones. Leather wrapped and lace presented, my body is finally my playground again. I bar the gate. I open the door. My choosing, over and over, every time. My word that always means stop. My pleasure marked with a bold X. My carnival sideshow redemption.

"Let me be your houseboy, just for a week," she says. "Let me show you my tricks." I come home from work the next day to find my bath drawn and fragrant, a mix from the top of my pile of tapes playing, a bowl loaded on the coffee table next to a glass of ice water, the temperature of everything showing precision as well as presentation. Showing that she is paying attention.

She oils her strong, small hands and slides them around my neck, fingers curling into the sore spots to the point of protest, then release, and my head is suddenly light; my shoulders drop, and I relax back into the V of her thighs. Perching on the thin rail of perfection, breathing it in together. "Don't let your bath get cold," she says, and I slip into floating petals and candlelight.

Two days in, she decides to try some role-play, which I usually love, but picks an Italian male persona and plays it well, which means seduction becomes spat and my bath is cold when I finally shut myself into the bathroom to have forty square feet of alone time. Too much arrogance, too many reminders of dangerous evenings babysitting. Too real. Not really her, not really her fault.

We curl up, smoke, talk, relax. We rope that character off, find our way back onto the same sweetly crooked page, smooth out the startles and uncertainty. She stays a full week and another. She is kind and generous and sexy and soon to cross the country for who knows how long, and yet. I want more quiet and fewer questions.

I'm still sounding out the dimensions of single. Wary of patterns, of possessive moments, of default plans. I treasure the pirate love notes and found treasures, the deep pools of passion. I indulge in bondage and belly laughs, braid charms into her shaggy punk cut, take her as far down as she wants to go. She's joyful but increasingly jealous.

I am lit up like a sparkler over this beautiful butch in my women's studies class, and while I try to avoid the subject out of kindness, she just can't leave it alone. Her living at our house is becoming increasingly complicated as well as convenient, and her courtship takes on an edge after Dani stops by one afternoon, inadvertently interrupting the beginning of some play.

I open the door just a crack, being as neither I nor the room are entirely presentable. Her gaze goes from my face to behind my head, and I realize she's watching the empty sling swinging back into stillness. Having lost all possibility for downplaying my eagerness, I invite her to drop by again soon. Heat burnishes my face while the ice gathers behind me.

## SOSSITY CHIRICUZIO

We're all single, non-monogamous, honest. We're all following trails of pheromones, politics, and instinct and trying to get it right. Dani has more experience than both of us put together, and Storm and I share mostly the understanding of young outlaws, which is to say we respect the need for individuality and factor in the likelihood of stumbling. Still, feelings.

She is solitary by nature, but her boy self is falling for me, grasping out of fear, bruised when I pull away. When I light up for others. When I don't cajole her to stay a little longer. I pull her close, nuzzle up her scent, whisper sweet and dirty all the intimacy I can't turn into falling in love. Fall onto the bed instead. Goodbye bites bloom on my collarbone, her nape.

She leaves in her little white car, packed with porcelain clay and leather gear, dashboard full of sticks and stones and runes and bones. She leaves me sore, still feeling her clever fist twisting toward my heart. She leaves a scent of boot polish, sex, and sandalwood soap, and a perfect set of black-and-white marbled toys, marked with red glaze and every whorl in her fingerprints.

# Meditation in motion

Soft curls of amber, rising to wispy clouds on the ceiling, set whirling by my deep exhales. In, twisting green and rich into my lungs, counting to ten, and release. Out, pouring blue and flat onto the air, out and out until I feel the pit of my stomach, and again.

Back arched like a cat, and then curved like a bowstring, and breathing, and deeper. Skin raising tiny hairs like whiskers, feeling the floor approach and fall away. Feeling the air move and the sunlight falling slantwise and summer hot across my shoulders.

Toes point, flex, reach, write sonnets on the air about blue and breath and the leak of light around eyelids closed for focus. About smoke and the smiles of ancestors on the altar. About green and expanding past comfort into growth and not being afraid.

My arms are vines, are snakes. Are wrapped around my torso like every rib bone is a separate note of pain, rippling into a melody of release. Like snakes, they twine, they move away, they warn, they embrace. They stretch, and again.

One skin, enfolding it all. One mind, connecting to nerve endings. Discovering. Forgiving. No gaze to distort it, not even my own. Breath, bone, muscle, tendon, joint. In, out, flex, expand, release. Heartbeat like a love song. Deeper than anyone else will ever go.

# A twisting path

I am feeling more at home in my body and less sure in my direction with every new adventure. I had been so sure that college would be the road to get me out of poverty and into stability, that teaching would be the way for me to help change the world, but nothing looks like straight lines anymore. This city is not where I live while I finish college, before I go somewhere else. It's where I live. Where I find lovers and friends, sharing food and book lists and insights and political awareness and community resources. Where I am finding myself.

I'm still taking classes, but those happen around the edges of what feels like my real life. Working and making art and unpacking all the damage that has been done to me. All the damage I've done. I'm healing through BDSM, through co-counseling, through study, through example, through writing. I even tried group therapy, though that left me feeling both more broken and not nearly broken enough to complain in comparison to others. All the wrong buttons getting pushed.

I'm filling my home with plants and books and music, with color and magic and passion. I'm filling my skin with my own self, all the way up to the surface, with sensations that I choose. Just last week, Raelyn Gallina led a whole day of ritual here, with rosewater blessings and body piercings and a bell dance. Sam and I played drums while Mary danced in ecstatic spirals, eyes closed and chest pierced with temporary needles, dangling fruit swinging soft arcs of blood across her breasts.

The air was thick with endorphins and transformation, and the new steel ring through my navel was the only anchor keeping my feet on the ground. Everything gleaming with energy and excitement and connection, we all shone like starlight and embers. Several lovers were there, but my desire was all for me. The feel of the metal in my flesh, my limbs moving through the air, my hair brushing my back, the velvety chill of chocolate gelato sliding down my throat, my hands pounding against the drumhead pounding rhythm against me.

Today, that same steel ring is warm against my belly as I drowse in the sling, sunshine slanting through the front window and Led Zeppelin playing softly on the tape deck. I am thinking about the coming months and where they might lead. I am thinking about love, how many forms it's taken in my life, how much easier it flows when I don't cling or hide or settle. I am thinking how much I miss my family and how quickly it changed from sharing my life with them every day to every once in a while. I am thinking that I have so much still to learn.

I feel those musings begin to coalesce into the mix of urgency and melody that is a poem trying to happen. I'm learning to accept these interruptions of my day as the gift they are, to find at least a moment to write down the seed of it on whatever paper is close at hand. I unfold them later, decipher my own code of emotion and imagery and metaphor, coax them into bloom. Looking for ways to tell my truths, to name my needs, to understand myself, to explain myself. Words are becoming my map, though I'm still not sure where it leads.

# About the author

Sossity Chiricuzio is a queer femme outlaw poet, a working-class crip storyteller. What her friends' parents often referred to as a bad influence, and possibly still do. She writes as activism, connection, and survival, and is half of the performance duo Sparkle & truth.

Her work has also appeared in a variety of publications including *The Rumpus, Salty, Adrienne, Argot, Lunch Ticket, F(r)iction,* and *Gertrude,* and anthologies like *The Remedy: Queer And Trans Voices On Health And Health Care, Glitter and Grit: Queer Performance from the Heels on Wheels Femme Galaxy, Not My President,* and *Leather Ever After.*

Find more online: sossitywrites.com, and @sossitywrites.

# Special thanks to

My mother, who remains my biggest role model in how to be true to myself, and how to help save the world by being an outlaw. My siblings, who never let me doubt my value as an outlaw in the world, and their lives. My unicorn of a partner, who inspires and encourages me every day. My Lambda cohort and mentor, who reflected the best parts of me as a writer and shared their insights and perspectives and stories so genuinely and lovingly. Bob & Sue, my generous "out-laws," who lent me their beautiful home for a writing retreat where this book was born. Every teacher who took my challenges in stride, and taught me nonetheless. The many healers who have kept my body going over the years. Every poor/working-class femme writer who ever carved time out of an impossible schedule and shared their poetry and stories – creating mirrors and antidotes and love notes that have saved my life. Damien Luxe and Leah Lakshmi Piepzna-Samarasinha who made time to read this book through and offer brilliant and kind feedback. Beaten Track Publishing, for taking a chance on a late-start writer with lots to say.

# Acknowledgments

Portions of this book were workshopped and written at the Lambda Literary Retreat in 2015, and during a Sou'wester Artist Residency in 2017.

# Previous publication credits

"Nowhere to go that is quiet," "Mermaid practice," and "The house that crumbled" were published as "The Florida years" in *Emerge: 2015 Lambda Fellows Anthology*.

"Research" and "Monsoon" were published in *Vine Leaves Literary Journal*, Issue 12.

"My high school sweetheart" was published in *Glitterwolf*, Issue 8.

"We need the dream," "Tired of have not," and "Monsoon" were published as "Mapping coordinates of poor, queer and feminine in the high desert air" in *Lunch Ticket*, the Summer/Fall 2017 Issue.

*All contents copyright Sossity Chiricuzio, all rights reserved.*

For more titles from Beaten Track Publishing, please visit our website:
https://www.beatentrackpublishing.com

Thanks for reading!

www.ingramcontent.com/pod-product-compliance
Lightning Source LLC
LaVergne TN
LVHW010317070426
835507LV00026B/3426